SURVEILLANCE UNLIMITED

*How We've Become
the Most Watched People on Earth*

Keith Laidler

ICON BOOKS

Published in the UK in 2008 by
Icon Books Ltd, The Old Dairy,
Brook Road, Thriplow,
Cambridge SG8 7RG
email: info@iconbooks.co.uk
www.iconbooks.co.uk

Sold in the UK, Europe, South Africa and Asia
by Faber & Faber Ltd, 3 Queen Square,
London WC1N 3AU or their agents

Distributed in the UK, Europe, South Africa and Asia
by TBS Ltd, TBS Distribution Centre, Colchester Road
Frating Green, Colchester CO7 7DW

This edition published in Australia in 2008
by Allen & Unwin Pty Ltd,
PO Box 8500, 83 Alexander Street,
Crows Nest, NSW 2065

Distributed in Canada by
Penguin Books Canada,
90 Eglinton Avenue East, Suite 700,
Toronto, Ontario M4P 2YE

ISBN: 978-1840468-77-9

Typeset in Sabon by Ellipsis Books Limited, Glasgow

Printed and bound in the UK by Butler & Tanner Printers

SURVEILLANCE UNLIMITED

CONTENTS

Part 1: The Watchers

Part 2: Tyranny's Shopping Basket

Part 3: Do We Need It – Do We Want It?

Dr Keith Laidler has a background in anthropology, and is also an acclaimed producer of wildlife documentaries. He writes regularly for the *Guardian*, the *Independent* and the *New Scientist*, and his many other books include *The Talking Ape* (Collins), *The Divine Deception* (Hodder Headline) and *Female Caligula* (Wiley).

Those who would give up essential Liberty, to purchase a little temporary Safety, deserve neither Liberty nor Safety.

Benjamin Franklin (1706–90)

The true danger is when liberty is nibbled away, for expedience, and by parts.

Edmund Burke (1729–97)

Sed quis custodiet ipsos custodes?
(But who will guard the guardians themselves?)

Juvenal (c. 60–130 AD)

A Fable For Our Time

Place a frog in a saucepan of very hot water and its survival instincts are activated immediately: the back legs unflex explosively and throw the amphibian clear of danger.

Place that same frog in a second saucepan of lukewarm water. Safe in its chosen element, and comforted by the pleasant warmth of the surrounding medium, the amphibian will choose to remain where it is. Now gradually increase the temperature, degree by slow degree, and a strange thing happens. The frog gradually habituates to the increasing heat until it will happily tolerate the temperature which made it leap from the first saucepan.

Stranger still, the amphibian will choose to remain in the steadily heating liquid – provided the temperature is raised slowly enough – until, one by one, its vital functions begin to fail. Eventually, it is boiled alive: overcome by the stealthy approach of danger.

Politicians in Western societies have taken this lesson of incremental advance towards a chosen goal to their hearts. Denied the simplicities of rule by diktat, they have applied it to the human population under their charge in a bewildering variety of fields; from taxes and creeping privatisation, through education, to increasing EU federalism and foreign invasions. Nowhere has this stealthy approach to increasing state control been more successful than in surveillance and the destruction of our liberties and privacy.

Part 1

THE WATCHERS

Only those with something to hide have something to fear.

Anon

If one would give me six lines written by the hand of the most honest man, I would find something in them to have him hanged.

Cardinal Richelieu

1

A Day in the Life of
the Database Citizen

Thursday

10.40 AM:
John Brown is returning by plane from a business trip to Germany. He booked at the last minute with a colleague, but the pair asked not to sit together, as they both prefer window seats.

This seemingly innocent request flags them up on Project Semaphore, part of the UK government's e-borders programme which screens and records everyone entering and leaving the United Kingdom. It will soon include all 40,000,000 domestic plane and ferry journeys, providing a comprehensive passenger movement audit trail that can be checked against other databases.

11.10 AM:
On landing, John heads for passport control, passing Mobile Forward Looking Infra Red (FLIR) cameras whose job is to remotely search beneath passenger clothing for hidden weapons or drugs.

The queues remind him of the doubts he's been entertaining about a planned family holiday to Florida's Disneyland. Since

9/11 and the 'war on terror', visiting the States requires a lot more than a simple passport. Under the US-VISIT programme, launched in 2004, every visitor must be fingerprinted by a US Customs and Border protection officer, who also takes a digital photograph of the traveller's face. John doesn't like the idea of a foreign country in possession of his family's biometric data, and wonders if they wouldn't have just as much fun at Disneyland Paris. Unfortunately, EU regulations will soon demand identical biometrics on passports and ID cards.

John is right to be concerned. According to a recent comprehensive report, US authorities use biometric identifiers to confirm the identity of passengers so that their details can be checked against over a dozen mega-databases including those of the FBI and Interpol.[1] What he does not realise is that his own trip to Germany has already been logged in various European databases, including the giant Schengen Information System (SIS).

12.00 NOON:
As he leaves the airport, John hardly notices the numerous CCTV cameras that record every aspect of his passage through the building; indeed, some cameras are so carefully blended with the airport décor that they are impossible to make out. A number of these machines use automatic face recognition to check for identity on passport and driving licence photo databases. Once the Identity Card scheme goes 'live', such intrusive surveillance will be rolled out countrywide, and all public anonymity will vanish. Even citizens who eschew all domestic and international travel will be instantly identifiable to the gaze of the CCTV operator.

12.11 PM:

On the way to his car, John phones his wife Irene to say he arrived OK, and mentions jokingly that 'there was no Al Qaeda attack on our plane'. This conversation is immediately picked up by an Echelon satellite through the keywords 'Al Qaeda' and 'attack'. All telecommunications traffic in Europe and the rest of the world – phone, mobile, fax and email – is listened in to by the Echelon system, which is run by the US National Security Agency. Three major optical networks, each carrying 100,000 calls, have been routed by BT into the US base at Menwith Hill near Harrogate. John's conversation is recorded and transcribed for analysis by human operatives. As a precaution, a trace is put on his mobile.

12.21 PM:

After speaking with his wife, John leaves his phone switched on, which enables the watchers to triangulate his position from nearby mobile phone masts as he drives into his central London office. But even with the phone off, the mobile can be remotely activated to send in its position-data every five minutes or so. Every mobile, on or off, can be made to function as a tracking device.

12.45 PM:

London confuses John and he resorts to satellite navigation, or 'sat nav', to find the best route to the office, not knowing that the GPS system, which is run and owned by the American military, can use the equipment to track his movements. Sometimes John parks his car outside central London and uses his Oyster card to travel in on the tube. Each time he does this, his every move is watched by Transport for London's extensive CCTV system, and his Oyster card automatically logs his identity and movements, giving the authorities a detailed travel trail over several weeks, should this prove necessary.

2.15 PM:
John was needed at the office only for an hour or so, and is soon back in the car heading for home. The petrol gauge is showing empty, so he pulls into a service station where a forecourt camera, linked to the police-operated ANPR (Automatic Number Plate Recognition) system, reads his number plate and compares it to a database of 'targeted' number plates of vehicles wanted in connection with criminal or terrorist activity. John's office also lies within the Congestion Charging Zone and, despite the charge being levied only between 7.00 am and 6.00 pm, his car registration plate, like that of every other car entering the zone, is logged day and night by another ANPR camera. The cameras used are similar to those that are sited every 400 yards on all major motorways in the UK, all reporting directly to a police command centre.

3.15 PM:
During their earlier phone conversation, John's wife had asked if he would pick up their sixteen-year-old son Mark from school. As he gets into the car, Mark tells his father he's just been fingerprinted 'to speed up the lunch queue', so joining at least 1 million children in the UK who have now had this biometric taken, often without parental consent.

John is annoyed that no opportunity was given to opt out of the scheme; a biometric cannot be changed, and if a hacker breaks the school computer Mark's ability to obtain a driving licence, credit facilities or a passport will be compromised for life. He's also worried about the possibility of 'planted' finger-prints leading to wrongful arrest. Just six months earlier, John himself had come face to face with the injustice of the UK's new biometric regulations – he was wrongly identified by CCTV footage as a shoplifter and had both his fingerprints and DNA sampled. Despite proving his innocence, neither biometric has been removed from the police database, and both will remain there even after he is dead.

4.00 PM:

On the way home John and Mark decide to stop off at a shop-ping mall to buy some wine and soft drinks to celebrate John's return. The car is tagged by CCTV as it enters the car park, and the registration number read and logged. Other cameras watch his movements throughout the city centre; citizens in London can have their image captured 300 times in a single day. John's gait and movements around the city centre are auto-matically analysed for 'suspicious behaviour' by algorithms in the CCTV software.

4.15 PM:

John uses a credit card, automatically establishing a further link in the transaction trail that records his every purchase, date and location in real time throughout the year. And he also uses a reward card, whose purchasing details are sold to marketing companies. John has been buying Anusol™ for haemorrhoids, and the reward card information is used to put him on a haemorrhoids database (they do exist, along with others for equally embarrassing ailments such as incontinence and erectile dysfunction!). Very soon now, John will be receiving unsolicited promotional brochures through the post detailing a revolutionary new piles treatment he might wish to buy. Every economically active individual in the UK appears on around 700 databases.

5.00 PM:
Back in the car, and Mark is already texting friends on his new mobile phone. John bought the device on the understanding that they would also use it to employ a company specialising in tracking mobile phones. With this service, he'll always know where Mark is. Thanks to the alert that his 'Al Qaeda' message initiated, all phones linked with John have been included in the watch on him, so Mark's texts are also being subjected to detailed scrutiny.

7.15 PM:
After dinner, safe in the comfort of his own home, John spends the evening surfing the internet, where numerous 'cookies' inform the search engine of every website he has visited, how many pages were read and for how long. The information generated will be sold to marketing companies and, combined with his store and credit card purchase details, means that John's doormat will soon be covered with an even bigger pile of unwanted junk mail. Outside the house, drone mini-helicopters with CCTV watch from above, while infra-red enabled cameras turn the dark night into day. As John and his family sleeps, newly deployed Visibuilding technology will soon allow police to scan through the walls of his home, and those of all his neighbours, to locate each person in any room of the house, and observe their most intimate behaviour.

2

SOMEONE TO WATCH OVER ME

In the days following the attack on the Twin Towers, liquor-store owner Akram Jaber was driving his $50,000 Chevy Suburban along Chicago's south side when he was stopped at gunpoint by two men and carjacked. As his attackers drove off, Akram reported the theft to the police, then called an operator at OnStar, a company offering a GPS service, including stolen vehicle tracking. The OnStar operator asked only his name, registration number and four-digit PIN. With these details he was able to immediately locate Akram's vehicle via a satellite link, and to order the satellite to update the car's position every minute. He then sent the GPS coordinates to the waiting police dispatcher, who quickly coordinated the capture and arrest of the carjackers and returned the stolen vehicle to a surprised and satisfied Akram, who commented that 'the police were amazed at how easy it was'.[1]

A clear example of the benefits of satellite vehicle location? Perhaps, but this same apparently benign technology can just as easily monitor the entire car-owning population of the United States, criminal or not; it can track dissidents in China, environmentalists in Canada, reformers in Zimbabwe, indeed anyone anywhere, whether or not their cause is just.

Ex-Home Office minister John Denham's outburst against the dangers of our 'sleepwalking into a surveillance society' and former prime minister Tony Blair's desire to establish a single multi-faceted national database have brought into focus the many dangers to privacy and personal freedom now facing our modern techno-civilisation. Denham's concerns are with the proliferation of government databases, something Blair and his successors wish us all to embrace in the name of efficiency and security, but this topic merely scratches the surface of surveillance techniques presently in use, or soon to be deployed. Satellite tracking of your car, video auto-identification of your features, surveillance of your emails and faxes, listening in to all your telephone conversations, and covert surveillance via transmitters implanted in your clothes, via your switched-off mobile and via your credit card transactions. The profiling of your character, needs and interests by surveillance of every website you visit, every newsgroup you scan, every purchase you make. And the correlation of every one of these pieces of data, and more, into a comprehensive 'life-log', a searchable 'Google' of each individual in society.

This is no futuristic Big Brother scenario: the technology exists now to do all of these things. Some are initiated and controlled by government. Others come pre-installed on your computer. Still more are being quietly fitted into articles and garments you may purchase, ostensibly to aid 'commercial marketing practices', though they retain the potential for less innocuous purposes (Windows XP allows for the remote activation of your webcam and microphone). There are no longer any technical barriers to a surveillance society.

A recent survey of 10,000 EU citizens found that privacy protection came high on their list of concerns. Orwell's *Nineteen Eighty-four* warned of the perils of an all-knowing, all powerful elite; today's surveillance is less overt, but just as real and in many ways even more pervasive.

We are confronted here with a Janus Technology and we must

decide which way we want it to face. Surveillance may well help in the fight against terrorism and organised crime, and aid in increasing productivity and efficiency in the workplace. But at what price? If the cost of zero carjackings is zero freedom, are we willing to pay the market rate? Is the deployment of such technologies even legal under our present laws? What will be their effects on the fabric of society? And what can we do to prevent the worst excesses of 'surveillance unlimited'? The surveillance web has become so complex that few people understand even a small part of the issue. The potential for abuse is far-reaching and formidable.

There are benefits and there are downsides, but while the former are magnified and celebrated, the dangers inherent in the system are routinely de-emphasised or ignored, and the ability of this technology to invade every aspect of our lives is never considered in its frightening entirety. The discourse and informed debate necessary in a free society has simply not taken place. Nor can it, when the information is not readily available to the public. It is time to take stock of 'surveillance unlimited' and to ask just where this huge proliferation of innovative, and largely unknown, technologies may be leading.

The All-Seeing Eye

You are a prisoner confined within the walls of the grim Panopticon, an enormous circular penitentiary laid out like a giant bicycle wheel lying on its side. Your cell is one of hundreds, perhaps thousands, lining the inner side of the wheel, row upon row and column upon column, completely covering the inner wall. The sides, floor, ceiling and outer wall of your cell are made of solid concrete, while the side facing inwards is essentially transparent, composed of an iron grid fastened across its length from floor to ceiling. At the centre of this gigantic structure, where the axle of the wheel would be located, is a screened glass turret affording a 360-degree view of the cells, and allowing whoever is in the turret secretly to watch the activities of every prisoner via a number of telescopes. This is the domain of the Inspector, the undisputed ruler of the Panopticon.

The Panopticon, or All-Seeing Eye, is no futuristic dream, but the plan of a model prison drawn up by the 18th-century Utilitarian philosopher and theorist of British legal reform, Jeremy Bentham.[2] Designed to function as a 24/7 surveillance machine, the crucial aspect of the Panopticon was mental uncertainty: because the prisoners could never see the Inspector (and Bentham envisaged partitions and blinds within the tower so that not the slightest noise or flash of reflected light should reveal the identity or activity of the Inspector), they could never know when they might be the object of scrutiny. A network of communication tubes of labyrinthine complexity, which would almost certainly have been too elaborate for the construction skills of the 18th century, allowed each prisoner to hear – though not reply to – the dictates of the Inspector.

The Panopticon is in reality an elaborate exercise in mind control, an enclosed world in which every aspect is designed to give the illusion of constant surveillance.[3] To impress this belief on the inmates' minds, Bentham further suggests that minor infractions of the rules may be ignored by the Inspector for several days, encouraging the prisoner to commit further, more serious misdemeanours. Then, on some completely arbitrary date, the anonymous Voice from the communication tube should proclaim to the prisoner his list of past sins, and the punishments that will follow. The inmates 'henceforth become aware that impunity is an illusion, that even silence on the part of the Inspector means only that he has chosen ... not to intervene yet'. Like God, the Inspector moves in mysterious ways, all-knowing and yet unknowable, and able at any moment to bring down inescapable retribution on the heads of his charges. The result of this elaborate theatre is to internalise the rules and regulations pertaining to the inmates' behaviour. If crime *always* leads to punishment (because one is always watched and can do nothing without being observed) then a form of self-discipline arises where criminal tendencies are suppressed and it is no longer necessary to punish. Or so Bentham believed. The French philosopher Michel Foucault summarised the implications of 'Panopticism' in his seminal 1975 work *Discipline and Punish: The Birth of the Prison*:

> Hence the major effect of the Panopticon: to induce in the inmate a state of conscious and permanent visibility that assures the automatic functioning of power. So to arrange things that the surveillance is permanent in its effects, even if it is discontinuous in its action; that the perfection of power should tend to render its actual exercise unnecessary; that this architectural apparatus should be a machine for creating and sustaining a power relation independent of the person who exercises it; in short, that the inmates should be caught up in a power situation of which they are themselves the bearers.

Total surveillance producing total (internalised) obedience. For Bentham, the Panopticon concept was a social panacea that cured many of humanity's ills:

> ... morals reformed – health preserved – industry invigorated – instruction diffused – public burthens lightened – Economy seated, as it were, upon a rock – the Gordian Knot of the Poor Laws are not cut, but untied – all by ... Architecture.

Replace 'Architecture' with 'Surveillance' and Bentham's concept has a chillingly familiar ring to it. All the pious aspirations enumerated in Bentham's breathless 'puff' have been cited as benefits that increased surveillance will bring. Note too that Bentham's 'Architecture' is in reality a technology that allows a total surveillance environment, and the parallels are even more compelling. It may be argued that the Panopticon is a prison, which immured its subjects in discrete cells, preventing any freedom of movement. But this was simply a necessity of the times. Given the technology that Bentham was forced to work with, the Panopticon was his solution to the problem of rehabilitating 'deviant behaviour' using total surveillance. If more modern technology obviates the need to hold the subject in a given area, yet provides as much information about his or her whereabouts and activities – and, as we will see in these pages, it can do just that – is the subject any less spied upon? If there is no escaping the gaze of the Inspector, are we not correct in considering every individual so closely watched as to be effectively nothing more than a prisoner in a very open prison?

A New Panopticon?

Surveillance has become something of a dirty word in modern society. But surveillance is by no means a new problem, nor is it inherently evil. We are all quite happy to be looked after or watched over in a variety of risky situations, for example by lifeguards at a swimming pool, by air traffic controllers, or by coastguards surveying marine traffic. Children are routinely watched over by parents and carers. Indeed, we are constantly under 'surveillance' by our family and close friends. They are privy to information not vouchsafed to the general population on such topics as our health, financial stability, employment, religious affiliation, and political and sexual orientation. This is an inevitable part of the social contract which we, as humans, tacitly agree to live under. We will, however, tolerate only so much scrutiny. When 'surveillance' is not a voluntary part of our own interpersonal schedule, for example in the case of 'small-town' inquisitiveness or the lack of privacy in intimate communities, such prying is often resented.

To a large degree, this is a question of consent, and a matter of power. When we hold a dinner party, we grant our friends the right to view the inside of our homes, to see what books are on our library shelves, which magazines and newspapers we subscribe to. Over the meal we allow 'interrogation' on our politics, environmental concerns and religious views. There is consent and an equality of power here; or rather, power lies with the homeowners, as a guest can always be asked to leave.

What disturbs most people is the covert, involuntary scrutiny of our private lives by large corporations or government departments which are, by their very nature, both anonymous and more powerful than any individual they may choose to target. Not that this has ever stopped such prying – surveillance has been part of human behaviour for over 5,000 years.

3

BIG BROTHER HAS ALWAYS BEEN WATCHING

Spying and surveillance are at least as old as civilisation itself. The rise of city states and empires, and their almost continual rivalry, meant that each needed to know not only the disposition and morale of their enemy, but also the loyalty and general sentiment of their own population. In the Old Testament we find the story of Joseph, who was sold into slavery in Egypt by his half-brothers and rose to the position of Vizier at the court of Pharaoh. When his brothers visit Egypt to buy corn, Joseph accuses them of being spies looking for weak points along the Egyptian border. Later Moses, after leading the Israelites out of Egypt, but before entering Canaan, sends out spies 'to bring back a report about the route we are to take and the towns we will come to.'[1] The Book of Numbers gives additional details of the information the spies were required to collect:

> See what the land is like and whether the people who live there are strong or weak, few or many. What kind of land do they live in? Is it good or bad? What kind of towns do they live in? Are they unwalled or fortified? How is the soil? Is it fertile or poor? Are there trees on it or not? Do your best to bring back some of the fruit of the land.
>
> (Numbers 13:17–20)

Alexander the Great's military success came as much from surveillance prior to a campaign as from his tactical genius in the field. But he was as interested in monitoring the dispositions of his own men as those of the enemy, and introduced a number of innovations to obtain this intelligence. He is known to have established one of the earliest postal espionage systems in around 334 BC, and to have secretly opened outgoing letters from his soldiers – probably history's first mass mail intercept. Any soldier whose writings questioned Alexander's authority was sent home to avoid possible treachery or mutiny.

Around 350 years earlier, the Assyrian Empire spent much of its time and resources spying on its rivals. Among the well-preserved ancient archives in Nineveh and Nimrud, there are many cuneiform tablets which reveal the existence of secret service networks used by the Assyrian court to communicate with provincial officials during the 8th and 7th centuries BC. One of these letters (Letter 380 – Ashur-risua to King Sargon), from an Assyrian agent sent to report on conditions in border states, gives an intriguing insight into surveillance reports from nearly 3,000 years ago:

> To the king my lord, your servant Ashur-risua. May it be well with the King my lord.
>
> Three thousand foot soldiers, prefects and chieftains of Sietini the governor ... have set out for the city of Musasir. They have crossed the Black River. His pack animals, the herd of Sietini, is before him.
>
> Regarding Sunai ... I have heard it reported his men have set out also for the city of Musasir.[2]

Such early societies are characterised by relatively harmonious vertical relations between classes, connecting patrons with clients in a deferential social hierarchy. The king bestowed his favour on his nobles, who in turn bestowed their largesse on a descending order of social inferiors. Horizontal relations (i.e. within a given social stratum) tended to be based on rivalry, with each individual vying for the favour of their immediate social superior. Although peasants' revolts and their like were not unknown, patronage ties tended to weaken many forms of group mobilisation. Furthermore, given the relatively low level of technological sophistication, and the difficulty of communicating quickly over long distances, such societies tended to fragment into a mosaic of smaller power blocs, each centred around a single individual – a baron, earl or warlord – and a specific geographical location. Except in times of war or insurrection, the mass of people in such a society were left very much to themselves, with little or no oversight from whatever central government might exist.[3]

Societal scrutiny did of course exist. The local noble would have his spies and informers; the temple or church would be aware of the peccadilloes and opinions of its parishioners; and peer pressure to conform with local norms of behaviour and belief was usually very efficient at stifling non-conformist attitudes or uncovering any whiff of rebellion, fraud or scandal. But all such scrutiny was opportunistic and local. The idea of a surveillance net covering the entire nation and subjecting each individual in that nation to routine, detailed scrutiny was not only inconceivable at that time; it was an administrative impossibility.

The rise of the modern nation state swept away such intermittent, parochial forms of oversight and ushered in an order of government that has culminated in today's surveillance society. Especially in the West, the growth of central state power is linked inextricably to the birth and expansion of capitalist institutions based on the primacy of the market. As capitalism flourished, its wealth-making potential resulted in a bonanza of tax revenue for the equally fast-developing state bureaucracies, and helped consolidate a centralised system of power. In addition, the success of free market economics led to a substantial class of affluent industrialists and merchant adventurers whose presence, and laissez-faire philosophy, helped in no small measure to undermine the traditional basis of society.

These factors, conjoined with the emerging industrial revolution in the late 18th and early 19th centuries, dramatically altered social relations. More and more of the population were crammed into increasingly large and depersonalised factories and cities, creating what Michael Ignatieff memorably described as a 'society of strangers'.[4] In such circumstances the old face-to-face social sanctions, and their seeming corollary, arm's-length rule by a relatively weak central government, simply would not work. A new set of social relations evolved, resulting in the establishment of a series of institutions now very familiar to any member of a Western liberal democracy: to the tax collector and (intranational) military groupings was added the police, prisons, regular censuses and a general flourishing of state bureaucracy, all of which required a constant and increasing flow of data on the manifold aspects of the individuals now securely under their charge.

In the case of the European democracies of the 19th century (though we should bear in mind that such democracies normally denied suffrage to the female half of their population), a reasonable compromise between the power of the state and the autonomy of the individual was reached, with elections, policing by consent, and not too detailed a scrutiny by the bureaucracy of individual behaviour. An Englishman's home was recognised as his castle, and his right to do what he wanted, when he wanted, free from the prying eyes of the state, was a basic tenet of the social contract. As historian A.J.P. Taylor observed:

Until August 1914 a sensible, law-abiding Englishman could pass through life and hardly notice the existence of the State, beyond the post office and the policeman. He could live where he liked and as he liked. He had no official number or identity card. He could travel abroad or leave his country for ever without a passport or any sort of official permission. He could exchange his money for any other currency without restriction or limit. He could buy goods from any country in the world on the same terms as he bought goods at home.[5]

In countries with a more autocratic system, where toleration of dissent was minimal, the rise of a national bureaucracy shaped a far more forbidding society. In contrast to England's freedoms, Russian society in 1914 was dominated by the *Okhrannoye otdeleniye* (which translates as Security Section or Security Department), usually called the Okhrana, a secret police force of the Russian Empire tasked with protecting the Czar and hunting down elements hostile to the state; these included revolutionaries, socialists and trade unionists, both at home and abroad. Voluminous files were kept on every conceivable suspect, including poets and writers, the data were collected using undercover agents, and constant surveillance of suspects occurred, including 'perlustration', the interception of private correspondence.

The Okhrana were dissolved after the 1917 February Revolution, though its functions were essentially taken over by the equally fearsome NKVD. Indeed, with the coming of the Age of Dictators, both Stalin and Hitler greatly extended and strengthened state surveillance of their respective populations. Such excesses, courtesy of the KGB (formed in 1954), continued in Russia after Stalin's demise. And they were taken to extremes in the German Democratic Republic (better known in the West as East Germany) where the GDR's secret police, the Stasi, developed one of the most intensive authoritarian surveillance regimes the world had yet seen. This was based not upon sophisticated computer-driven analysis, but on paper files and a huge number of paid spies, estimated to include an astonishing one-sixth of the total population of East Germany.[6]

Totalitarian excess apart, bureaucracies the world over have always longed to know what their citizens were doing and thinking. Sometimes this inquisitiveness has valid governmental reasons, such as logistics, forward planning and security, and sometimes it is purely for control. Moreover, researchers such as Maria Los have described the 'unintentional totalitarian effects' flowing from contemporary developments in risk management and social sorting.[7] Any administration will keep records, and will almost invariably arrogate to itself the right to engage in covert surveillance – phone tapping, mail interception et cetera – should this be deemed necessary for the security of the state. While these powers are certainly necessary during times of danger (and have been, for the most part, subject to relatively strict judicial control, at least in Western countries), they are undoubtedly open to abuse, as the recent history of the USSR, East Germany, North Korea and numerous other autocratic states attests.

However, no matter how repressive those totalitarian regimes, their attempts to control and observe every aspect of their citizens' lives were always foredoomed to failure. Motivation was not lacking, but the technology was. It was simply physically impossible to open every letter sent, to listen to every telephone conversation, to know where every person was at any given time of the day, what each individual in the society was interested in, what newspaper they read, what subjects attracted their attention. Even if such complete surveillance had proved possible, *collating* all these disparate facts into useful and usable information was quite simply beyond the capacity of the human brain.

The Tyrant's Dream

The advent of electronic intelligence, banking and communication has swept away all such limitations. It is now possible, indeed it is easy, to follow any given individual; to listen in to their telephone conversations, read their email, track their movements within a city or an entire country, and to form a profile of their lifestyle, preferences, hatreds and political affiliation. Indeed, much of this is already being done on a routine basis.

The legal structures necessary to prevent abuse lag far behind the deployment of these powerful new technologies. In addition, the perceived or manufactured threat from Al Qaeda and related terrorist cells has softened resistance to their introduction. There is a pressing need to examine the wide nexus of surveillance technologies now in our environment, and those soon to be deployed, most of which remain effectively unknown to the public at large. We also need to determine what we must do to put in place effective firewalls against an unacceptable level of surveillance (much of which, if performed by human operatives rather than covertly by a machine, would raise a storm of protest), and what actions must be taken to prevent misuse of these systems and forestall the undoubted potential for the introduction of tyranny by stealth.

Most people will discount the possibility of a despotic regime arising in Western culture. But then again, in the early 1930s few envisaged Hitler's meteoric rise to power, the mass executions, concentration camps and genocide. In a 2007 radio interview Yoko Ono told how, as a child of wealthy parents in 1930s Japan, she attended a birthday party at which a fortune-teller had been provided to entertain the children. The first child to test the seer's powers was given a grave prognostication; the fortune-teller predicted that the boy would suffer great tragedy and lose everything. The children laughed the seer to scorn for his warning, for the boy was heir to one of the most wealthy families in Japan. 'It was ridiculous', Ms Ono recalled. 'For our friend to lose everything Japan would have to lose everything, and we could never see that happening ... Then the War came.'[8]

Suspend disbelief for a moment, and consider the possibility of an authoritarian regime, or a fully-fledged dictatorship, arising in any of the Western democracies. How would such a regime seek to maintain itself in power? Let us look at a hypothetical tyrant's shopping-basket – a 'Christmas list' of the equipment and networks a would-be dictator would most desire in order to guarantee knowledge of all his subjects' behaviour and attitudes, and total control of society. We can divide the list into six main headings:

IDENTITY
The master key to collating personal information – a cradle-to-grave individual number for each member of society

LOCATION
The ability to locate, watch, identify and track any individual in real time

COMMUNICATION
The ability to intercept all types of communication

LIFESTYLE
The ability to determine any individual's true likes and dislikes by monitoring interests, purchasing biases and entertainment preferences; this category includes confidential knowledge of any individual's financial or health status, etc

CORRELATION
The ability to cross-reference all this data to form a comprehensive profile of each member of society

ACCEPTANCE
Acquiescence to or, even better, non-awareness of the above surveillance among those subject to it.

Quite a challenge for Santa but, as we'll see in Part 2, a by no means impossible task in our computer-centred, web-based, credit-card-carrying society.

Part 2

TYRANNY'S
SHOPPING BASKET

None are more enslaved than those who
falsely believe they are free.

Goethe

4

IDENTITY: THE NEW IDENTITY CRISIS

According to Lawrence Lessig, professor of law at Stanford University, 'a system of perfect identity is a system of perfect control'. The rationale for this statement is obvious. If it is possible to identify each individual in every situation by a single, unique reference number, then it is much easier to construct a surveillance picture of that person's whole existence, from major life data such as health or financial status all the way down to the smallest details of their dietary habits or fashion preferences. It has long been acknowledged that perfect identity is the single most important condition for the establishment of a controlled society, and so central is this principle that Portugal, Austria, Germany and Hungary have constitutional limitations on the establishment of a national numbering system.

The best safeguard against this threat is a degree of bureaucratic inefficiency within the state machinery. As long as you have a government structure composed of a variety of departments, each of which allocates to an individual different identity codes, then communication between these departments will remain difficult, and all the information concerning an individual is unlikely to be collated. While such confusion does have its drawbacks – it allows the establishment of dual (or more) identities and a whole range of fraudulent activity within banking, health and social services – it also holds Big Government at arm's length. Bureaucratic chaos is the shield of privacy.

The United Kingdom's planned identity card scheme, and similar projects worldwide, will change all that.

ID cards

The true nature of the ID card was revealed by former Tory minister Peter Lilley, whose Cabinet revolt led to the abandonment of a former Conservative government's ID scheme. 'There is', he said, 'no policy that has been hawked, unsold, around Whitehall for longer than identity cards … It was always brought to us as a solution looking for problems.'[1] For at least the past 50 years, the state bureaucracy offered the idea to every new incumbent of the Home Office, and most turned it down flat. Then, as Philip Johnston memorably describes in the winning essay of the 2007 Charles Douglas-Home Memorial Trust Award, '… along came a Labour government, David Blunkett and September 11, a toxic combination that the Home Office had been looking for. The dust was duly blown from the plan rejected by the Tories and resubmitted to the Blair administration, duly tweaked to reflect the latest justification for its disinterment with the added lure that played to New Labour's modernistic fetishism: biometrics.' ID cards suddenly became the answer to a host of social problems, from terrorism through benefit fraud to immigration. And civil liberty concerns went out of the window.

The controversy surrounding ID cards concerns much more than the issue of whether or not we should be forced to carry a simple plastic card in our purse or wallet. The card is essentially the tip of a surveillance iceberg, the visible peak of a multi-layered identity management mountain which is to be imposed on every adult legally resident in the UK. At its centre sits the National Identity Register (NIR), a giant database that will hold at least 50 pieces of information on each ID card-holder, although more can be added at the discretion of the home secretary, and will allow government agencies to collate information on everyone with a card. There will be a legal requirement to provide, and update, all registrable facts, with criminal sanctions for non-compliance (see p. 77). The data will be shared between government departments, and perhaps other organisations, on an unprecedented scale. The NIR is effectively an index to all other official and quasi-official records, through cross-references and an audit trail of all checks on the Register. The database would be the portal, and a none-too-secure one at that, which gave access to a total life-log of every individual, from the time of first registration until death. In fact it could be even longer than that; records would be kept on file indefinitely.

In December 2006, the then home secretary Dr John Reid gave notice that the NIR database would not now be built – instead, he said that the data would be divided between three existing UK systems: the national insurance, asylum and passport databases.

A victory for privacy advocates? Not quite. This was more political grandstanding than a real change in government attitudes to the surveillance society. Computer systems can now be networked so effectively that it is immaterial that the data is to be held on three geographically distant systems. What we have here is a 'virtual NIR', whose ability to access and correlate these vast amounts of data will be unimpaired.

'Real' or 'virtual', there are two main objections to the NIR. The first, as was ably shown by the information commissioner's report 'What Price Privacy?', is that the Civil Service's planned merger of all its databases, combined with the NIR (which is set to hold, as the commissioner points out, 'identifying information, residential status, personal reference numbers, registration and ID card history, as well as records of when, what and to whom information from the register has been provided'), will create a frighteningly efficient tool of surveillance. The second concern relates to just who will be able to access this 'mother of all databases', and what safeguards there will be put in place to prevent the input of incorrect information. The government is not renowned for its IT competence: there have been monumental cock-ups at the Criminal Records Bureau, the Child Support Agency, the National Health Service, Immigration Service and a host of others. As early as 1994 the then President of the Law Society of England and Wales, Peter Williamson, was voicing his scepticism: 'I'm not convinced that the home secretary really believes that the database and its supporting technology will be faultless and that mistakes will not occur. I doubt that anyone could be convinced that this level of perfection would exist in a government-led initiative.'[2] An individual would not be aware that his record has been mislabelled, or incorrect data added, until his or her life suddenly fell apart. Nor would a citizen know when and by whom their records had been inspected.

And these are legal intrusions into our life. Criminal activity is another matter altogether. Information commissioner Richard Thomas's report reveals that government databases, such as DVLA and health records, are all regularly breached. This is not surprising. The Police National Computer has 10,000 entry points, which makes breaching the system child's play for computer literate criminals and others who may profit by gaining entry. In one instance, the Information Commissioner's Office (ICO) obtained warrants that led to a house in Hampshire, where a private eye had unfettered access to the police database, the DVLA's records and BT phone records. Once all state databases are linked, it will be that much easier to 'surf' records in a host of government departments, and to amass a multi-tude of facts on any individual, including vital, lifetime-relevant biometric identity data.

Identity check

There are many ways for an individual to establish identity, but they can all be conveniently subsumed within the following four categories:

1. Something you have, e.g. a card
2. Something you know, e.g. a PIN
3. Something you do, e.g. handwriting or signature
4. Something you are, e.g. fingerprint, iris or retinal pattern.

This latter category are 'biometric traits', which are in essence any measurable physical or physiological characteristic or behavioural traits that can be stored on a database and used to recognise, authenticate or verify the claimed identity of any individual. For example, the national DNA computer data-base, launched in the UK in 1995, will eventually contain the genetic fingerprint of most of the country's population. As the Home Office website proudly proclaims, over 3.5 million people, '5.2 per cent of the UK population, is on the database compared with 0.5 per cent in the USA'.[3] Thanks to the mapping of the human genome, DNA profiling allows an ever-increasing vista of the individual's health, ethnic origin, susceptibility to specific diseases, sensitivity to certain environments, and perhaps even sexual orientation, to be detected on the basis of a simple blood or saliva sample. The UK government has made known its preference for keeping DNA samples of everyone arrested by the police on file indefinitely, even those who are subsequently found innocent. Such a database lays the foundation for mass surveillance and social engineering on an almost unimaginable scale. Along with 'profile' information on lifestyle, it could be used to ascertain health care and insurance entitlements, and 'appropriate' categories for employment.

Other examples of biometrics include iris scans, retinal scans, voiceprints, palm vein recognition, and – currently planned for the UK identity card – facial morphology and fingerprints. Strictly speaking, 'biometrics' refers to the automated systems that measure and confirm identity, but the word is increasingly used to designate both the hardware and the physical characteristics themselves.

Most biometrics follow a two-stage system. In the first stage, Enrolment, a biometric sample is taken from an individual; an iris scan, perhaps, or a fingerprint. A full fingerprint image requires a large amount of disc space and often, in a process analogous to computer compression procedures, specific data is extracted to form a biometric template, unique to that image. Whether full image or template, the data is stored using either a central database or a 'distributed environment', such as smart cards. It is only in the second stage, Comparison, that the biometric system becomes useful. Anyone presenting themselves to the system will be asked to submit the relevant biometric characteristic. The system then compares the submitted sample with the stored sample(s). Should there be a match, the identity of the individual is confirmed, or 'accepted'. Without an acceptable match, the computer 'rejects' the individual and denies entry.

Biometrics offer government an almost foolproof identity check – at least for law-abiding citizens. With criminals and terrorists it's another story. Counterfeit cards are already a reality, and Professor Tsutomu Matsumoto has recently demonstrated just how easy it is to fool a state-of-the-art iris reader with a simple laser printout. The same researcher has also blown a very large hole in fingerprint biometrics by successfully fooling the scanner using equipment that was neither hi-tech nor particularly expensive. Matsumoto took latent fingerprints from a glass and enhanced them with superglue. The resulting image was photographed with a digital camera, the contrast enhanced using Adobe Photoshop, and the fingerprint image, now darker and much better defined, printed onto a transparency sheet. Then, using a cheap, photosensitive printed-circuit board (PCB) – easily obtainable from electronic hobby shops – Matsumoto used the fingerprint transparency to etch an image into the copper of the PCB. With this as a mould, he prepared a gelatine 'digit' with a usable fingerprint, which fooled fingerprint scanners 80 per cent of the time. Matsumoto later discovered that the children's candy 'Gummi Bears' was an acceptable substitute for gelatine. Other methods have also been shown to give acceptable results.[4]

Fingerprinting children

Despite Matsumoto's success in circumventing biometric gateways, the UK government is pressing ahead with plans to collect data on iris scans, DNA, fingerprints and others across the entire population. Perhaps the most scandalous attempt to obtain biometric information by stealth has been the wholesale fingerprinting of children in the United Kingdom, a practice which the People's Republic of China, amongst others, has banned.

Immigration minister Liam Byrne confirmed in early 2007 that the government is considering setting up a database of fingerprints of children aged eleven to fifteen, as part of the preparations for the introduction of biometric passports and ID cards. The excuse for this draconian measure was unconvincing.

Ministers were said to be concerned that young people between the ages of sixteen and twenty, if they held a child passport issued between the ages of eleven and fifteen and valid for five years, could end up travelling for a period on passports without biometric details. Mr Byrne said:

> The challenge that officials have been asked to find an answer to is how do you make sure that people who are sixteen and over have got biometric details recorded in their passports? If you only have to renew your passport every five years then potentially a twelve-year-old won't have to renew their passport until they are sixteen. That would mean you would have some sixteen-year-olds who would have a passport without biometric details.

Shock! Horror! So we are being asked to believe that the government – who have no qualms in accepting thousands of adult asylum seekers and migrants from some of the most unstable parts of the world, many holding non-biometric passports of dubious authenticity – are suddenly 'concerned' that a few sixteen-year-olds with valid passports may pose a security risk by holding those (valid) passports without biometrics for a year or two. Is this an example of twisted priorities, or are we looking at something far more worrying?

Opposition spokesmen certainly seem to think it's the latter. The then Liberal Democrat home affairs spokesman, Nick Clegg, was outraged: 'The government's determination to build a surveillance state behind the backs of the British people is becoming increasingly sinister ... It is a measure of ministerial arrogance that plans are being laid to fingerprint children as young as eleven without having a public debate first.'

Shadow home secretary David Davis was equally scathing: 'This borders on the sinister and it shows the government is trying to end the presumption of innocence ... With the fingerprinting of all our children, this government is clearly determined to enforce major changes in the relationship between the citizen and the state in a way never seen before.'

According to the *Sunday Times*, the Identity and Passport Service (IPS) envisages fingerprinting 295,000 children aged between eleven and fifteen who apply for passports in 2010, with the number rising to almost half a million annually. In an interview with ITV's *The Sunday Edition*, Byrne stated that no final decision had yet been made on whether to go ahead with the proposal. But it appears that there may be a 'Plan B' already in operation – fingerprinting children, some far younger than eleven, at school.

My first acquaintance with this new means of obtaining biometric data began when I happened to see a crumpled brown envelope in the bottom of my sixteen-year-old son's school bag. The letter informed me that my child would be fingerprinted some time within the next few days. I was mildly perturbed at this sudden arrival at our school of a practice normally associated with identifying criminals, and took it upon myself to look a little deeper into the situation. What I found both appalled and frightened me.

More than 3,500 schools had already begun fingerprinting their pupils; it was estimated that around 750,000 children had already been processed and their biometric data consigned to school databases (today's figure is over 1 million). Children as young as three years old were being fingerprinted; some were told by their teacher that it was a spy-game, and not to tell their parents. There was a wholly unjustified 'assumed opt-in' to the scheme – letters were sometimes sent informing parents that fingerprinting was about to occur, or that it had already occurred. Often, there was simply no letter. Government funding worth 50 per cent of the total cost was available for installation of the fingerprinting system, while none was offered for comparable non-biometric methods such as swipe cards. And yet a former home secretary managed to both claim ignorance and bestow tacit approval on the process in the House of Commons. Jack Straw, then Leader of the House, in responding to requests to devote parliamentary time to the issue, stated that 'I am not aware of the practice, but obviously people have accepted it.'[5]

A letter to my son's headmistress elicited further information. She informed me that the local authority were actively promoting the scheme, and had informed the school, as had the company selling the equipment, that the data collected was not a fingerprint; the deputy head had earlier told me that the scan was 'merely a series of numbers, not a fingerprint'. She therefore did not feel she was fingerprinting any pupils and had no qualms about introducing the scheme, which would speed up lunchtime queues in the cafeteria. She'd also been informed that the 'template' that each child gave of their fingers was not compatible with police or government databases. Nor would she allow 'fishing expeditions' by the police or anyone else:

> We do not usually suffer from 'fishing expeditions' and never give access to our database to outsiders, even the police. If they need information I make a judgement about whether to give it or not and then I give it in a personal meeting to an Inspector.

The protection of all fingerprint data at the school complied with local authority and Education Department standards. The implication was that I was overreacting.

Unfortunately, a lot of savvy computer experts also seemed to be as worried as I was. Although I am sure that the information our head teacher vouchsafed was given with the best will in the world, and with no intention to mislead, very little stands up to detailed scrutiny. To take her points one by one:

FINGER SCAN IS NOT A FINGERPRINT

Contrary to the scanner manufacturer's claims, the experts insisted that the template was a fingerprint in all but name. In May 2007 Kim Cameron, the architect of identity and access in Microsoft's connected systems division, explained how it works:

> If you want to find out who owns a fingerprint, just convert the fingerprint to a template and do a search for the template in one of these databases. Call the template a binary number if you want to. The point is that all you need to save in the database is the number. Later, when you come across a 'fingerprint of interest', you just convert it to a number and search for it. Law enforcement can use this information – and so can criminals.

Andrew Clymer, an identity management security expert who has spent more than eight years at Cisco Systems, providing clients such as Fidelity and Merrill Lynch with secure network environments, agrees:

> The fact that the fingerprinting system does not store the actual print as a picture is irrelevant. The fact that it is able to compare an input against this number and determine a match is the critical issue. It does not seem beyond the bounds of possibility that by understanding what the vital points are you should be able to manufacture a print that exhibits these points. The burden of proof has to be that this couldn't be done in a person's lifetime.

And of course, with exponential advances in technology, no one can seriously make such a claim. In fact, German researchers recently claimed to have reconstructed full fingerprints from just such data.[6]

SCAN NOT COMPATIBLE WITH OTHER SYSTEMS

It turns out that there are international standards to ensure that biometric templates from different manufacturers are compatible; so, data that is stored on one system can be read by any other, including government systems. The M1 system (otherwise known as INCITS 398 or NISTIR 6529 – the latter, intriguingly, partially sponsored by the US National Security Agency) allows for fingerprint templates from different manufacturers to be compatible and interchangeable:

> The Common Biometric Exchange Formats Framework (CBEFF) was devised by industry and US government representatives and describes a set of data elements necessary to support biometric technologies in a common way. These data elements can be placed in a single file used to exchange biometric information between different system components or between systems. The result promotes interoperability of biometric-based application programs and systems developed by different vendors by allowing biometric data interchange.[7]

'FISHING EXPEDITIONS' BANNED

Nor, with the best of intentions, could any head of school prevent a police fishing expedition. By virtue of the Regulation of Investigatory Powers Act 2000 (RIPA), data can be viewed on the grounds of national security, preventing or detecting crime, preventing disorder, public safety, protecting public health, or in the interests of the economic well-being of the United Kingdom.

Moreover, the legal situation can change at any time. On 2 October 2007, home secretary Jacqui Smith sanctioned a massive increase in government access to personal data, allowing the phone records of every person in the United Kingdom to be legally scrutinised by a host of government departments: the tax office, the Food Standards Agency, the Department of Health, the Immigration Service, the Gaming Board, the Charity Commission, and – most incredible of all – the local council. While none of these bodies will be able to actively listen in on phone conversations, each of them now has the right to know when and where you called, say, Alcoholics Anonymous, The Samaritans or any other confidential support service, a political party or action group, even a premium rate kinky chat line. Given the cavalier manner in which such sweeping powers have been granted by the home secretary, how can any teacher or school governor be sure that the fingerprint data they have taken will never be seized, quite legally, by an arm of the government?

Protection of data

This is of critical concern as, should biometric data on any child be stolen, that child's privacy and security is compromised for, quite literally, as long as they live. In the future, it seems inevitable that fingerprint data will be used to authenticate bank accounts, passports and other important 'life portals'. Information security consultant Dom Devitto is adamant that '... the value of this information, and the length of time it has this value, is high ... I would never condone holding large amounts of biometric information on almost any school site.' Microsoft consultant Kim Cameron is even more scathing:

People have to be stark, raving mad to use conventional biometrics to improve the efficiency of a children's lunch line.

This extremely valuable biometric data on around 1 million
schoolchildren (around 15 per cent of the total school population) is currently held in ordinary school PC systems, and is
under threat from a number of sources, as we shall see.

CYBERTHEFT

School systems can be hacked, as has been proved on numerous
occasions. And as the number of uses for biometric data increases,
especially in banking and other financial services, the motivation
and rewards resulting from a successful breach of any school's
security will skyrocket. As Andrew Clymer explains, security
experts tailor their measures 'so that the estimated time required
to crack the security makes the data redundant. In this case
however we are talking about a person's lifetime, and once
broken there is no possibility of changing the underlying data as
this is based on an individual's biometrics.'[8]

Much biometric data is encrypted, but again, the value of
this information to a thief makes it worth going to extraordinary lengths to crack the code. The data may even be held
secretly for years, as data can be stolen without leaving any
detectable sign that a breach has occurred. The value of biometric
data will not diminish until the originator of the biometric dies,
and can be quietly cherished by its new 'owner' until such time
as computer advances allow access to it. It is alarming to discover
that the German Enigma code of World War II can be easily
breached with today's ordinary home PC. Today's state-of-the-
art technology is tomorrow's museum piece; the 64-bit DES
(Data Encryption Standard) developed in 1976 by the US
National Institute of Standards and Technology has already
been cracked on today's supercomputers.

Andrew Clymer has eloquently described the problem for school biometrics:

> Can I seriously make a bet today that the information will remain secure for a lifetime? I don't believe any IT security expert would be able to make such a guarantee – and especially in these cases on a shoestring budget.

SIMPLE THEFT

Schools are broken into in the UK on a weekly basis, and the prime target for the thieves is computer equipment. A school in Yorkshire suffered the theft of a computer containing details of 260 pupils.

VULNERABILITY OF BACK-UP STORES

It is likely that any school using biometrics will take routine precautions and back up its data, to avoid a systems 'crash' and consequent upheaval in re-enrolling its student population. As Dom Devitto points out: 'This has to therefore pose the question of where the backup media will be stored, and how easily it could be lost or stolen – or worse, simply sold – without anyone really noticing.'

RECONSTRUCTION FROM DISCARDED PCS

As fraudsters and paedophiles have discovered to their cost, simply hitting the 'delete' button on your computer's keyboard does not completely erase the unwanted or incriminating data on the hard drive. In order to be absolutely certain that the data cannot be retrieved, the hard drive itself needs to be physically destroyed. Clymer cites the case of 'a university forensic science course [which] purchased a number of hard drives from eBay and then used a variety of tools to extract the data from used blank drives. In a sample of twenty such drives they found a sex offender, two schools' pupils databases and a customer list from a mobile phone shop.'[9] It is absolutely essential that all schools using biometric systems employ the services of a professional data cleanser.

Rufus Evison, consultant to a number of computer industry bodies, has cited a further danger; that of illegal acquisition of data at the interface between the child and the scanner or reader:

> Claims that the child giving a fingerprint in an insecure area cannot result in identity theft is reminiscent of the claims that the banks used to make in the early days of cash machines. Now of course we know to look out for additions to the cash machines that strip our cards and so allow access to our bank accounts. Perhaps schools need to train teachers in the technology thoroughly enough that they can spot non-standard hardware concealed behind the library computers?[10]

The irony is that many schools defend using biometric systems for reasons of efficiency and finance. Each fingerprint reader costs around £25,000 to purchase. Add to this the cost, including time lost in training staff to put the system into effect, and it is obvious that economics is not an issue and that some other factor is driving the burgeoning use of child fingerprinting. With *The Times* reporting on leaked government plans to fingerprint children between the ages of eleven and sixteen and to hold the information on a secret database, with the intention of processing around half a million children annually by 2014, the strategy behind school fingerprinting is not hard to fathom.[11]

Legality and human rights

Strangely, for a system that has already been deployed in up to 17,000 schools,[12] the legality and human rights aspect of fingerprinting children remains far from clear. The Information Commissioner's Office (ICO), while urging, though not insisting, that schools consult parents before collecting fingerprints, has not come out against the practice. In January 2007 David Smith, the deputy information commissioner, commented: 'For us to come out now and say fingerprinting isn't allowed would be very difficult because these systems have come in over the last four years.' Which is, to say the least, an extremely ambiguous position. Is the ICO taking the position that fingerprinting of children is a bad thing, but because the cat is already out of the bag they've decided to let it continue? Such an attitude could set a very dangerous precedent, and serves merely to emphasise the image of the ICO as a toothless sham, its existence owing more to PR than to real concerns over privacy protection. By contrast, Privacy International's view, namely that the practice of fingerprinting for the purpose of library cards (or lunch queues) was in clear violation of the Human Rights Act and the Data Protection Act, is unequivocal and based on strong evidence: 'The law states that privacy invasion must be proportionate to the threat. A few lost library cards do not warrant mass fingerprinting', said Privacy International's Simon Davies. It is also likely that the practice breaches Article 16 of the UN Convention on the Rights of the Child, which says that 'no child shall be subjected to arbitrary or unlawful interference with his or her privacy ...'

Privacy International believes that fingerprinting 'dehumanises our children and degrades their human rights', and along with other campaigning organisations such as Leave Them Kids

Alone, has called for the unconditional withdrawal of the technology from schools.

Perhaps the most insidious result of this low-profile mass fingerprinting of Britain's children is the effect it will undoubtedly have on the children's perception of biometrics. Is this – along with the establishment of a fingerprint database by stealth – the cover for New Labour's support of a system that must, to all reasonable people, be the prime exemplar of taking an enormous technological hammer to crack a small logistical walnut? Simon Davies of Privacy International is on record as stating that 'the use of such systems will have the effect of desensitising people to more comprehensive privacy invasion – such as ID cards and DNA testing – later in life ... Such a process has the effect of softening children up for such initiatives as DNA testing and ID cards.'

The ID fiasco

The proposed ID card system certainly needs all the help it can get. Privacy International compiled a survey of problems with ID cards from correspondents in 40 countries. The problems were legion, but they came up with twelve main reasons why ID cards are a bad idea:

1. Won't stop crime or terrorism
2. Won't stop benefit fraud
3. Won't stop illegal immigration
4. Will facilitate discrimination
5. Will constitute an unwarranted increase in government powers
6. Will become an internal passport
7. 'Voluntary' card will become compulsory

8. The cost will be unacceptable
9. Loss of card will produce great distress and inconvenience
10. Will imperil the privacy of personal information
11. Will entrench criminality and false identity
12. Will compromise national integrity and personal identity.

It is worth looking at these topics more closely, as the first three have been used extensively as a rationale for introducing ID cards, and the remainder are carefully de-emphasised or avoided altogether in government proposals.

1 WON'T STOP CRIME OR TERRORISM

There is no evidence to show that the presence of a comprehensive ID card system has in any way been a significant deterrent to terrorist acts. Former home secretary David Blunkett has acknowledged that ID cards won't stop terrorism, as two-thirds of all terrorist offences are carried out without the aid of false identities. ID cards for homegrown terrorists, such as the 7/7 London tube bombers, are an irrelevance that distracts from better and cheaper means of prevention. And past experience suggests that, where there is a need for false ID, competent criminals and extremists alike will find ways to subvert the system. Indeed, too great a reliance on the presumed infallibility of an ID card, which can in fact be forged, could actually diminish security.

2 WON'T STOP BENEFIT FRAUD

An ID card may help prevent a small proportion of the more blatant false identity claims, but this should be placed in perspective. False identity costs are estimated at just 2.5 per cent of all fraudulent claims (i.e. £50 million of a total £2 billion per

47

year). Not a very good return for the almost £20 billion estimated as needed to set up and run the system over the next ten years by an LSE report.[13] Even the government admits a (rising) cost of £5.61 billion.[14]

3 WON'T STOP ILLEGAL IMMIGRATION

The appalling traffic in humanity certainly needs strong control measures, but people-smugglers will pay no more heed to ID cards than they do to present-day visas and passports. The majority of migrants originate from developing nations, countries whose poverty will preclude access to generally available biometric and/or RFID identity cards. So, short of banning entry to all citizens of developing nations, foreign nationals will still enter the UK using genuine or forged 'paper and picture' documents from their supposed country of origin.

4 WILL FACILITATE DISCRIMINATION

Using proposed powers, a home secretary could classify the UK population into a number of groupings and make registration on the NIR of such a category mandatory. People may be classified by law under religious affiliation or ethnic group, or such information may be determined without their knowledge by cross-referencing with other databases. Even the possibility that this might be happening could have grave consequences. As the chairman of the Bar Council has stated, 'is there not a great risk that those who feel at the margins of society – the somewhat disaffected – will be driven into the arms of extremists?'

5 WILL CONSTITUTE AN UNWARRANTED INCREASE IN GOVERNMENT POWERS

According to campaign group No2ID, 'without reference to the courts or any appeals process, the home secretary may cancel or require surrender of an identity card, without a right of appeal, at any time. Given that the object of the scheme is that an ID card will be eventually required to exercise any ordinary civil function, this amounts to granting the home secretary the power of civic life and death.'[15] We have another example of this in the new UK passport: anyone who is concerned about the amount of biometric information on the passport, and declines to submit even a single item of data, will not be issued a passport, and therefore will be effectively confined within the borders of the UK for life.

The 'checks and balances' in place to prevent abuse of power, that is to say the powers granted to the National Identity Scheme Commissioner, are risible in their inadequacy, like those designed to 'police' the Data Protection Act (see chapter 12). The National Identity Scheme commissioner will not report direct to Parliament, will have limited powers, and a number of key issues (e.g. the ability of the commissioner to investigate serious complaints) will be placed beyond his jurisdiction.

6 WILL BECOME AN INTERNAL PASSPORT

Many aspects of everyday life could become conditional upon ID card inspection by those in authority, from police and immigration officers to car park attendants and traffic wardens. Travel by train, air or bus may be likewise compromised; as a nation we are more used to hearing the words 'your papers, please' spoken in the cinema or on DVD by a Gestapo thug or an agent of the Stasi. Should various sections of the population be targeted disproportionately, as occurred in the hated 'stop and search' strategy of the 1990s, racial or religious tensions could well be exacerbated.

7 'VOLUNTARY' CARD WILL BECOME COMPULSORY

Privacy International's analysis, conducted in the late 1990s, was well-nigh prescient with regard to the UK's proposed ID system. Labour's 2005 manifesto stated that the scheme would be 'rolling out initially on a voluntary basis as people renew their passports'. Once in power, the Home Office undersecretary of state, Andy Burnham, doctored this commitment in a letter to colleagues, omitting the first part of the statement and claiming that 'we have a clear manifesto commitment to introduce the National Identity Register (NIR) and the identity cards scheme "as people renew their passports"'. Gone was the mention of any 'voluntary basis', and the way was clear for compulsory ID cards; the only voluntary dimension to this farrago was if an individual decided voluntarily not to travel abroad. Anyone renewing their passport, or applying for a new one, will soon be required to attend an interview at which all designated details must be submitted. There is no choice in this. In addition, the home secretary, at his or her sole discretion and without asking their consent, can add any person to the National Identity Register.

Campaigning Labour MP Lynne Jones took Andy Burnham to task over his blatant sophistry in a splendid letter that exposed New Labour's doublespeak with timely clarity. Having pinned the undersecretary of state to the floor over his scandalous omission of one half of the manifesto promise on ID cards, she goes on to say that he tries to '... get around the fact this was supposed to be voluntary by stating: "The manifesto reference that this would take place on a voluntary basis refers to the fact that no order setting out a date for compulsory enrolment would be laid in this parliament."'

Ms Jones goes on: 'How were voters supposed to know that? It is ridiculous to infer that this is what people would have understood ... Furthermore, the government made much of the fact that further primary legislation would be required before the scheme becomes compulsory ... There will be compulsion for ordinary people through [passports and other] designated documents, compulsion which will not come through the "front door" of primary legislation.'

The full letter is a jewel of precision in the face of government obfuscation, evasion and downright lies, and deserves to be read in its entirety.[16] It makes plain that despite recommendations against a National Identity Register by expert panels, despite cost estimates based on flawed and wildly optimistic projections, and despite concerns that the ID card scheme will be socially divisive and actually increase identity fraud, the government was pushing forward, by stealth, with implementation of a compulsory scheme whose only beneficiaries will be bureaucrats, and those intent on hacking into what the chief technology officer for Microsoft UK has called a 'data honeypot' for criminals.

8 THE COST WILL BE UNACCEPTABLE

The UK government claims that the cost of the ID card scheme will come in at just under £6 billion. How this figure has been arrived at is anyone's guess; the shadow minister for home affairs, Edward Garnier, was scathing: 'I rather suspect that the United States Congress got more candour out of the Pentagon on the projected costs of the stealth bomber than we are getting out of the government on costs of this particular IT project.' Experience with earlier civil service IT projects suggests that the costs will be more than double or treble the initial estimate (see examples cited on p. 53). Industry and public sector costs for complying with the new system, estimated to be at least double the total cost of implementation, have been ignored in the government figures, as have less invasive, low-cost and low-tech alternatives to the problem of national ID management.

Nor is the government keen on adding any extra detail. In February 2006, the House of Lords submitted amendments that, *inter alia*, would have required that the full costs of the

ID card implementation be estimated, the 'material assumptions' underpinning the estimate be made clear, and the resulting cost estimates be signed off by the Comptroller and Auditor General. In addition, the Lords' amendments would have required the government to state the intended benefits of the system, so that any claimed advantages could be subjected to proper scrutiny. The government was having none of it. Thanks to its majority of supine MPs, the amendments were rejected in two separate votes: 314 to 261 and 316 to 257.

A less 'spun' appraisal of the true costs of the ID project was made at around the same time in a London School of Economics report called *The Identity Project: An Assessment of the UK Identity Cards Bill and its Implications* (published June 2005). Six months in the making, its researchers spoke with nearly 100 industry representatives, experts and researchers in the UK and worldwide, under the guidance of a steering group of fourteen professors. Their 'high water mark' estimate for ID implementation was a massive £19.2 billion – over three times the government's own figure.

In January 2007, the then home secretary John Reid announced that plans to build the massive computer that was to house the NIR had been scrapped. This was not the whole story, however; instead, information will be held on three existing and separate systems: the UK's national insurance, asylum and passport databases. The government denied that the changes were a U-turn, claiming that the move would save money, lead to greater efficiency and lower the risk of fraud. Conservative party spokesman David Davis said: 'This is an admission of what will be a financial disaster for the taxpayer, with a cost-overrun of billions.' The then Liberal Democrat shadow home secretary, now leader, Nick Clegg was equally dismissive: 'These are sticking plaster measures in which the government is cutting corners to make the increasingly unpopular ID card scheme more palatable. The fact remains that however much John Reid rearranges the deckchairs, ID cards are doomed to be unacceptably expensive, intrusive and unmanageable.'[17]

9 LOSS OF CARD WILL PRODUCE GREAT DISTRESS AND INCONVENIENCE
As time goes on it seems inevitable that the ID card will be required to allow access to an increasing number of goods and services, for example public buildings and services, bank accounts and transport infrastructure. Civil service history is littered with costly IT failures – past government cock-ups have involved the Identity and Passport Service (a Home Office project), tax self-assessment, the Post Office, national insurance and the prison service.

In one particularly inept example of bureaucratic incompetence, the Home Office – sponsor and coordinator of the national ID card system – was slated by the National Audit Office for a scandalous 'waste of money' over an IT system which was supposed to provide a national infrastructure for the probation service. The project was more than 70 per cent over budget, and costs were still rising as the NAO reported. The Home Office was criticised for 'poor specification of expected outputs, weaknesses in service monitoring and inadequate control of purchases', and had 'underestimated the technical risks' of the project. And this, be it noted, for a system of relative simplicity when compared to the intricacies of the National Identity Register. Such a record makes it inevitable that an administrative project of the size and scope of the NIR will produce a large number of identification errors. Being misidentified may lead to loss of rights or false arrest; the least one might expect is a huge disruption in the day-to-day running of one's life until the matter is resolved.

10 WILL IMPERIL THE PRIVACY OF PERSONAL INFORMATION

There is concern that the ID card, as currently envisaged, will increase ID fraud by broadcasting far too much personal data indiscriminately, whenever it is accessed. 'Would you be happy,' asks Microsoft UK's national technology officer Jerry Fishenden, 'if online auction sites, casinos or car rental company employees are given the same identity information that provides you with access to your medical records?'[18] It is already possible to design cards that will provide only as much information as the person or organisation interrogating the card needs to know; there is, for example, no need for an off-licence or pub to be aware of your name, date of birth, address, or any other piece of information other than the fact that you are at least eighteen years old.

11 WILL ENTRENCH CRIMINALITY AND FALSE IDENTITY

It is telling that the USA and Australia, both of which rely heavily on a single reference source, are plagued by much higher levels of identity theft than the UK. Once the ID card has become the trusted 'gold standard' for identity verification, it will actually prove *more* useful to any fraudster capable of forging or in other ways circumventing the card's defences.

There is a further problem, potentially of much greater importance. On 18 October 2005, Microsoft's Jerry Fishenden warned that the British ID card scheme may result in 'massive identity fraud on a scale beyond anything we have seen before'. Fishenden says that the collection of all sensitive biometric data by government has incalculable security implications. 'Unlike other forms of information such as credit card details,' he says, 'if core biometric details such as your fingerprints are compromised, it is not going to be possible to provide you with new ones.'[19]

Fishenden pointed to the 'honeypot effect'. A nationwide cache of personal data, all in one place, would be a 'richly rewarding target for criminals ... [We] should not be building systems that allow hackers to mine information so easily ... Inappropriate technology design could provide new hi-tech ways of perpetrating massive identity fraud on a scale beyond anything we have seen before: the very problem the system was intended to prevent.'

12 WILL COMPROMISE NATIONAL INTEGRITY AND PERSONAL IDENTITY
The Home Office has been given the power to add information to the NIR, but has no duty to inform the individual concerned that such additions have been made. The data is arbitrarily considered to be accurate, but there is no criterion of accuracy; the legislation appears to make the incumbent home secretary the sole judge. Given that we already live in a 'dossier society', where bureaucrats prefer to work with the 'digital persona' within the computer rather than the real, flesh-and-blood individual, our personal identity will become in large part owned by the state and subject to the vagaries of bureaucratic procedure. In addition, there are indications that the government foresees future interaction between the state and private sectors, including business access to the National Identity Register, further endangering personal identity.[20]

Europe-wide ID

Not content with biometric ID cards in the UK, the British government, in a highly questionable move, used its presidency of the Council of the European Union to propose that biometrics (and RFID – see chapter 5) should be included in Europe-wide, standardised ID cards (this is EU doc no. 11092/05). The document claims that this measure is necessary to meet International Civil Aviation Organisation (ICAO) standards – again, see chapter 5 for more details. This same excuse has been used to introduce biometric data into both the UK passport and the proposed ID card. In both cases the government is being extremely economical with the truth. The ICAO standard requires only a digitised passport photograph – other biometrics, such as fingerprints, *are optional*, and are being added because the government specifically wishes them to be included, not because ICAO demands them. Moreover, despite the fact that article 18 of the current EU treaty (the Nice treaty of February 2003) explicitly precludes adopting provisions on 'passports, identity cards, residence permits or any other such document' (article 18.3, para 2), in December 2004 the EU adopted proposals to introduce biometric passports.

Passport to scrutiny

While there are still problems with public acceptance of the ID card idea, at least in the US and the UK, passports are a different matter and have excited little attention. But recent proposals from a little-known and unelected UN-affiliated group are being used as a pretext to turn the humble passport into a dream ticket for a surveillance society.

The ICAO has been given responsibility for developing global standards for passports and other travel documentation. This has grown directly from the United States' EBSA legislation (Enhanced Border Security and Visa Entry Reform Act), which demands stringent hi-tech passports from all countries enjoying 'visa-waiver' status with the USA. Countries which do not comply will lose their visa waiver privileges. The ICAO's current proposals would incorporate a single biometric (a digitised photograph) into the passport, but most worryingly of all, make them readable from a distance, even though nothing in the EBSA

County Council

Barrow Library

Customer ID: ********58261

Title: Surveillance unlimited : how we've
become the most watched people on Earth
ID: 38003033921685
Due: 29/11/2014,23:59

Total items: 1
08/11/2014 10:48
Checked out: 1
Overdue: 0
Hold requests: 0
Ready for pickup: 0

SS1

requires this. Such remotely-readable passports could easily become the gold standard of ID checking and an internal ID card by default. Civil liberty groups' requests to consult on this momentous proposal have been met with silence.

If these ideas are implemented in the USA, UK and globally, governments could neatly side-step the politically sensitive proposals for a high-tech national ID card. And if, as seems likely, such passports become the gold standard for identity verification, they will increasingly be demanded from citizens in their daily lives, supplanting less sophisticated items such as driving licences which currently satisfy this demand. Alternatively, the new passport might become a template for the production of new driving licences containing biometric information; in fact, this has already been proposed. Either way, these documents will become de facto ID cards with the potential to become monitoring devices, readable by government security agents, marketing men and identity thieves alike, from a distance and without our knowledge.

This hi-tech addition to the traditional passport is just one of thousands of applications for a new technology that has profound implications for every individual in our global society, a technology that goes by the rather innocuous title of RFID – Radio Frequency IDentification.

5

RFID: Big Brother in Small Packages

Bar codes are so much a part of Western consumer society that we hardly even consider their presence on most of the goods we buy, unless it is to bless them for speeding up the line in our local supermarket. We present our purchases at the checkout, there's an audible recognition 'beep' as each is scanned, and the checkout attendant tells us how much we owe.

The first bar code patent was registered on 20 October 1949 by Drexel Institute of Technology graduate students Norman J. Woodland and Bernard Silver. The technology languished for another two decades before any bar code standard was approved; even then, it took a further ten years before the technology began to take off, and by 1982 around 15,000 suppliers were in the loop. Just five years later that number had risen to 75,000, and use of these elongated zebra stripes has continued to grow until the present day, when they are all but ubiquitous in the marketplace. The reason for such phenomenal growth was that the technology was embraced by a number of large outlets, notably Wal-Mart, who realised how effective bar coding was as a means of managing inventory. Any supplier who didn't take up the bar code banner was dropped by the retailing giant – the little guys were dragged along on the coat-tails of the most powerful stores, with bar coding their only means of avoiding the mercantile axe.

However, the system has its limitations. Bar codes have low storage capacity; they do not represent a unique item, but rather a class of item – for example, they can designate a particular brand or size of washing machine, but not each individual machine in that group. As they are mostly printed on paper they lack durability; they can be read only when there is an established line of sight and at very short distances; each bar code must be read separately, one at a time; and there is no way of rewriting a bar code if a change is necessary – the best you can do is stick a new 'zebra-stripe' over the old one. But technology has once again ridden to the rescue of the retail business; the all-pervading bar code is now on its way out, superseded by an even more efficient means of tagging everything from peanuts to people – the RFID chip.

RFID (Radio Frequency Identification) is a generic term used for a system which transmits data on identity (normally a unique ID code, such as a 128-bit serial number) wirelessly, from a distance, using radio waves. Also known as contactless technology, they are essentially transponders (transmitters/responders) which are always listening out for a signal sent by a transceiver (transmitter/receiver), which is also known as a reader. Typically, the reader sends a signal which 'wakes up' the RFID tag, as the radio signal energy is used to power the chip, and receives the tag's identifying signal in return via a sensitive antenna. The data acquired by the reader is then passed on to a host computer which may run 'middleware', or specialist RFID software, to filter the data and extract useful information.

RFIDs come in three 'sizes' which correspond to the radio frequency they transmit on, allowing operators to choose a chip to fit their exact requirements:

Low Frequency (125–134 KHz) – at present these are the rarest chips, used to track both valuable assets and individual animals in zoological studies.

High Frequency (13.56 MHz) – these are used where medium-range reading of data is required. The chips can be accessed at distances of up to 1.5 metres, or more if more sensitive antennae are used.

Ultra-High Frequency (850–950 MHz) – these are capable of high reading rates at ranges of approximately 3 metres.

Two final distinctions should be mentioned. RFID chips can be read-only, with unchangeable information programmed into the device during manufacture (the so-called 'number plate' application); others are 'read-write' chips, where information can be added to the tag, or the entire data set written over with new information. Most chips are 'passive' and take the energy they need to respond from the signal sent by the reader. However, some RFID tags (the largest and most expensive, though prices continue to fall) are 'active', indicating that they contain their own battery and can therefore transmit at distances of 100 metres and more. This distinction may soon be redundant because, as we'll see in chapter 7, work is now in progress to use animal and human metabolic processes to supply the energy they need to function indefinitely as 'active' chips.

The technology itself is neutral, as is the case for most of the topics covered in this book. It is the uses to which the system is put that can become a cause of concern. In much of manufacturing and shipping, RFID tags are a blessing. They allow retailers to reduce inventory levels, are potent anti-theft devices and also show great promise in recycling and waste management. Retailing giants Wal-Mart in the US and the UK-based Tesco have already installed trial 'smart shelves' with networked RFID readers, in order to streamline working practice. Wal-Mart has now mandated RFID tags from all of its suppliers – and as occurred earlier with the introduction of bar code technology, those who do not make their goods RFID compliant will lose the Wal-Mart market, something that can mean life or death to most companies. We can expect to see a huge burgeoning of RFID scanning for these same commercial reasons, making the technology ubiquitous in our society. Where Wal-Mart leads the world quickly follows.

Unfortunately, the reasons that make the RFID chip so attractive to business also present a huge threat to both privacy and liberty. These minute computer chips/transmitters, less than half the size of a grain of rice, can be programmed with a multitude of biometric and other information about an individual, and freely accessed by any appropriate scanner. The privacy questions raised by RFID tags are truly momentous.

The more RFID tags are used, the cheaper they will become. And the cheaper they become, the more they will be used. At present the price of the tags is a closely guarded commercial secret, but it is estimated that they retail at around 25 cents, which is equivalent to 12.5p at present exchange rates. But at least one company, the aptly-named Alien Technology, has predicted that at production rates of one billion and above the tags will cost around 10 cents, or 5p. Once the price reaches 5 cents (2.5p) it will become economical for every item worth a dollar or more to be 'chipped'. Anything you buy that is more expensive than a chocolate bar will be designated with a unique 64- or 128-bit unique identifier, capable of producing at least 18,000,000,000,000,000 (eighteen thousand trillion) possible values, enough unique identifiers to number every object on the planet. Given this versatility, more and more uses for the technology are being suggested. RFID tags are washable and have already been sewn into clothing; car manufacturers are beginning to use RFID tags in keys to authenticate the user; Michelin plans to implant an RFID tag into every tyre it manufactures; the European Central Bank is considering adding RFID tags to banknotes, and there is even talk of tagging senior citizens' medication and food, so that with the OAP wearing a miniature RFID reader, the oldster's daily habits can be monitored remotely by a caregiver.[1]

This could lead to a series of unwelcome intrusions into an individual's private life. You may not be upset by the idea of stores flashing *Minority Report*-type personalised ads onto giant plasma screens as you enter a store and are immediately recognised by your tagged sweater – your prior purchases and financial status analysed and your future wants predicted – but tagged sweaters and tyres can be used to keep your movements under constant surveillance wherever there is an appropriate reader. These do not even necessarily have to be densely sited; in the case of cars, a reader at every exit and entry point to a given road would be quite sufficient. Meanwhile, tagged banknotes will, at a stroke, eliminate the last anonymous means of currency exchange.

So far-reaching are the implications of RFID tagging in consumer products, that a coalition of more than 40 consumer, privacy and civil liberties groups from at least nine countries, including the American Civil Liberties Union, Liberty UK, the Electronic Privacy Information Centre, Electronic Frontier Finland, and British think-tank The Foundation for Information Policy Research, have issued a joint call for a voluntary moratorium on RFID tagging 'until a formal technology assessment process involving all stakeholders, including consumers, can take place'.

Their position paper acknowledges the usefulness of RFID tags in many commercial situations, for example in the tracking of pharmaceuticals and manufactured goods, though they say that such tags should always be permanently destroyed before reaching consumers. The destruction of toxic substances is another area where RFID tagging would prove invaluable. Landfill sites could read tagged objects brought in for disposal (an obsolete computer, for example) and, rather than embedding a unique item-level identifier in the machine, the RFID tag would merely give generic data (equivalent to 'I am a computer manufactured by X, and contain the following toxic substances …'). There is no doubting the immense contribution to efficiency and waste management that this technology could make in these situations.

That said, the paper lists five attributes of the technology that could be used in ways that compromise civil liberties and the privacy of the individual:[2]

Hidden placement of tags: RFID tags can be embedded into or onto objects and documents without the knowledge of the individual who handles those items. As radio waves travel easily and silently through fabric, plastic and other materials, it is possible to read RFID tags sewn into clothing or affixed to objects inside purses, shopping bags and suitcases, and other personal items.

Unique identifiers for all objects worldwide: The Electronic Product Code, which is contained in RFID tags, potentially enables every object on earth to have its own unique ID number. These could lead to the creation of a global item registration system in which every physical object is identified, and linked to its purchaser or owner, at the point of sale or transfer.

Massive data aggregation: The deployment of RFID requires the creation of massive databases containing unique tag data.

These records could be linked with personal identifying data, especially as computer memory and processing capacities expand.

Hidden readers: Tags can be read from a distance, not restricted to line of sight, by readers that can be incorporated invisibly into nearly any environment where human beings or items congregate. RFID readers have already been experimentally embedded into floor tiles, woven into carpeting and floor mats, hidden in doorways, and seamlessly incorporated into retail shelving and counters, making it virtually impossible for a consumer to know when or if he or she is being 'scanned'.

Individual tracking and profiling: If personal identity were to be linked with unique RFID tag numbers, individuals could be profiled and tracked without their knowledge or consent. For example, a tag embedded in a shoe could serve as a de facto identifier for the person wearing it. Even if item-level information remains generic, identifying items people wear or carry could associate them with, for example, particular events like political rallies.

Faced with such a worrying host of potentially disastrous scenarios, the coalition calls for what might be termed a 'bill of rights' to control the continuing roll-out of RFID technology in almost every sphere of life. Their statement concludes that a two-part framework should be put in place:

1. All RFID applications must be subject to a formal technology assessment, undertaken by a multidisciplinary impartial entity, which should include a consumer representative.

2. Fair Information Practices (FIPs) should prevail throughout the RFID industry, including (at a minimum):
   i. Transparency – there should be no secret tag-reading, no secret databases. Individuals have the right to know when an item has been tagged, where the readers are located, and the technical specifications of the technology being used.
   ii. Individuals must be informed of the rationale behind any specific tagging procedure, and given clear notice of the purposes for which the information will be used. Only information strictly necessary for that purpose should be collected.
   iii. Those implementing any RFID surveillance are to be held accountable both for the use of the RFID technology and the resulting data. An accountability system must be established, with RFID users held legally responsible for any infraction of the proposed principles.
   iv. Databases, data transmission and access to the system must be protected by adequate security safeguards. 'These should be verified by outside, third-party, publicly disclosed assessment.'

Some practices are so fraught with privacy and civil liberty concerns that the coalition believes they should be outlawed. These include the use of RFID to track individuals, either directly through implants or through tagged clothing or other items, without their prior informed consent; any implementation of the technology which serves to reduce anonymity, including RFID-tagged banknotes; and pressuring of consumers to accept live or dormant RFID tags, or prohibiting consumers from both detecting tags and readers and disabling any RFID tags on items in their possession.

RFID proponents have countered such worries with a number of placatory statements, and suggested a series of technical fixes whose value is, to say the least, somewhat dubious. Despite manufacturers proposing a 'global RFID network' for their product,[3] the public has been told that there are simply not enough readers in the environment to allow for continuous tracking of individuals. The short answer to this is 'No, not yet'. We are, at present, at the very beginning of RFID deployment – if we value privacy we should be demanding a freeze on the establishment of potential networks, which will be much harder to dismantle once they have been set up. Even in the absence of such networks, readers sited at convenient 'choke points' (such as arterial roads entering a town, car parks, bus and rail stations) could cover any given urban environment, and provide an excellent surveillance picture of every RFID-tagged individual, which – if tagging becomes ubiquitous – means everyone. Reader units at retail outlet entrances and exits would add detail to the general picture.

Again, we are assured that the range of RFID tags is so small as to preclude any possibility of human surveillance. While it is true that some passive tags have ranges of 2.5 cm or less, most RFID devices designed for consumer use possess ranges of up to a metre. Given that readers can be seamlessly implanted into almost anything, including door surrounds, tiles and concrete, this 'short' range is obviously sufficient to allow identification at the 'choke points' mentioned above. And we can expect that technological advances will improve both transmission range and sensitivity of reception. Indeed, in certain surveillance situations (e.g. tracking an individual across the floor of a railway station with embedded readers), short-range tags are actually preferable, as their low transmission range would ensure that the 'target' could be located with pinpoint accuracy and would minimise interference with other tags.

It is simply not credible to state that RFID tags are too expensive to ever become ubiquitous – just think of hand-held calculators, personal computers and mobile phones, all initially expensive technology whose price crashed in the course of a few years. Or that the tags carry only a serial number; this number can, of course, be used as a reference number that connects to one or several databases containing information on the individual to whom that number is linked. This can all be updated as the tag transmits its data to every reader it meets: entered central London 9.15am; parked Bloomsbury Way 10.00am; at British Museum 10.20am; took the tube from Oxford Circus to Marble Arch 11.45am; entered Selfridges 12.10pm; lunch at ... and so on. Every detail of every human's daily activity could be entered and logged automatically via RFID tagging.

Despite these concerns, and the inadequacy of industry response, RFID tags are currently being quietly included in clothing and a range of consumer products (see chapter 8).

Some RFID manufacturers are planning to go even further. They do not see the need to tag the items or objects we own, but simply wish to 'RFID' each human directly. The US Food and Drugs Administration has recently approved Applied Digital Solutions' 'VeriChip', a passive RFID chip about the size of a grain of rice, for human implantation. After a local anaesthetic, the device is injected beneath the skin in the shoulder or upper arm, and (in deference to cosmetic worries) is said to be 'almost invisible' when correctly implanted. At the moment, the chip is being sold on its supposed ability to identify medical conditions in victims who are unconscious or in some other way unable to communicate with medical personnel. However, the chip requires a reader in order to give up its information, and it does not actually contain any medical data, but instead the by now well-known 'identification number' which allows those scanning to gain access to the person's database. Aside from the question of utility (unless every ambulance and hospital ward is equipped with a VeriChip scanner, how will the chip be accessed?) and the even more pertinent question 'Wouldn't a low-tech dog-tag do the job quicker and more easily?', mention of the ubiquitous 64-bit number should set alarm bells ringing all over the world. The chip is a *unique identifier*. If a sweater can be tracked via RFID so can a person, and while it is at least possible to remove the sweater at any time (though very soon now you will need to remove every article of clothing, thereby becoming instantly identifiable to the ever-present CCTV camera), a minor operation will be needed to remove the VeriChip. Applied Digital Solutions is aware of the potential: 'VeriChip can enhance airport security, airline security, cruise ship security, intelligent transportation and port congestion management', states its PR puff. 'In these markets, VeriChip could function as a stand-alone, tamper-proof personal verification technology.' Which is true; any business or government department (or criminal) can read your data without you even knowing you've been scanned, 'correlating one's ID number with their own set of criteria, hosted on their own remote server ...' Once the chip is implanted, you are effectively at the mercy of anyone with a scanner.

To enhance the sales potential, the 'warm and fuzzy' aspects of the technology are being rolled out first. Chip implants, it is said, will help health professionals, and those working with Alzheimer's patients and other forms of dementia. And to put a smile on your face there's even the story of a bar in Sunny Spain that hosts 'chipping nights' for its customers. According to Ananova.com,[4] and other reports, the Baja Beach Club in Barcelona 'has now turned Tuesday nights into Implant Night where guests can be chipped between drinking and dancing'. With a chip, clients can avoid queuing for admission, and can buy their drinks and snacks using the VeriPay system by simply passing their implant within range of a scanner. We can only hope that such a method of payment does not become widespread. Having personally seen muggers in Guyana cut the finger off a woman to obtain a particularly tight-fitting gold ring, there is little doubt that unauthorised (and unanaesthetised) removal of chips in the course of a robbery would soon become commonplace.

The stakes were raised early in 2006, when a security company in the USA implanted chips in two employees which allowed the pair easier access to company property. Although there was, in this case, no compulsion, the procedure does raise serious issues with regard to personal privacy and the power of the employer. With calls for comprehensive implanting of the entire population being debated on technology websites, we should all be aware of the potential for control inherent in this technology.

There are other risks. Possible adverse effects include tissue reactions, migration of the implanted chip, magnetic resonance imaging (MRI) incompatibility, electrical hazards, and infection. Worse still, and possibly ringing the death knell for this unwanted technology, it was revealed in September 2007 that several studies, from the 1990s to the present, have demonstrated that the implanted glass-encapsulated RFID transponders from companies like VeriChip could cause cancer in laboratory animals.[5] In 1997, German researchers found cancers which were 'clearly due to the implanted microchips' in 1 per cent of 4,279 chipped mice. A year later, an American study of 177 mice reported a 'surprising' cancer incidence of just over 10 per cent, while in 2006 French scientists discovered tumours in 4.1 per cent of 1,260 microchipped mice. The French study was one of six where scientists were not originally seeking to discover microchip-induced cancer, but noted the tumours in the course of other experimental studies. Because the French researchers recorded only the most obvious cancers, their paper cautions that 'these incidences may therefore slightly under-estimate the true occurrence'. Although it is easier to induce cancer in mice than in humans, the findings remain a cause of grave concern. Having reviewed the evidence, Dr George Demetri, director of the Center for Sarcoma and Bone Oncology at the Dana-Farber Cancer Institute in Boston, said that there were 'certainly real risks' in RFID implants. Dr Robert Benezra, head of the Cancer Biology Genetics Program at the Memorial Sloan-Kettering Cancer Center in New York, agreed. 'There's no way in the world, having read this information, that I would have one of those chips implanted in my skin, or in one of my family members.'

The manner in which these implants were passed as safe for human use also raises worrying questions. Approval for the VeriChip implant was given on 10 January 2005 by the US Food and Drug Administration (FDA). Before approval of any new product is granted, the FDA is required to review all perti-nent scientific and commercial literature. Did it know of the studies implicating microchip implants in animal cancer? Privacy advocate and RFID expert Dr Katherine Albrecht asked to see the evidence the FDA had used to grant approval, but the Administration declined to provide any details. She filed a Freedom of Information Act request and, after over a year of waiting, was informed by letter that there were no documents matching her request. Albrecht was incensed: 'The public relies on the FDA to evaluate all the data and make sure the devices it approves are safe – but if they're not doing that, who's covering our backs?'

She forwarded the evidence she had amassed to the news agency Associated Press. Even with big-time media taking up the cudgels the FDA still prevaricated, using the traditional bureaucratic stonewalling strategy that VeriChip correspondence was being kept secret to protect commercial confidentiality. AP filed a Freedom of Information request and the FDA finally rustled up Anthony Watson, who was in charge of the VeriChip approval process, for telephone interview.

Displaying a touching naivety in business matters, Watson claimed that the companies requesting approval are expected to provide data on safety 'even if it's adverse information'. Asked about the studies linking implants to cancer, he said that 'at the time we reviewed this, I don't remember seeing anything like that'. Equally improbable was the statement that the FDA's own literature search 'didn't turn up anything that would be of concern'.

Other questions remain. The FDA is overseen by the Department of Health and Human Services (HHS) which, during the time of the VeriChip implant approval, was headed by Tommy Thompson. In a disquieting twist it appears that, two weeks after the device's approval, Thompson left his Cabinet post and within five months was a board member of VeriChip Corporation and its parent company Applied Digital Solutions. According to the *Washington Post*, SEC (Securities and Exchange Commission) records reveal that Thompson received options on 166,667 shares of VeriChip Corporation stock, and options on an additional 100,000 shares of stock from its parent company, Applied Digital Solutions. He also received $40,000 in cash in 2005 and again in 2006. Asked about this frankly suspicious chain of events, Thompson denies any involvement in the approval process, and claims no personal relationship with the company he eventually joined, while the VeriChip was being evaluated. In a telephone interview with the *Washington Post* he claimed that he '… didn't even know VeriChip before I stepped down from the Department of Health and Human Services'. Verichip itself declined to comment. Thompson's underling, the FDA's Watson, stated: 'I have no recollection of him being involved in it at all.' Which is, of course, a very different thing from stating that Thompson was not involved.

The tag that dare not speak its name

Just as troubling is the largely unreported plan to place RFID tags into government ID cards. Not that the government will admit it in so many words, preferring to use that well-known ruse of re-branding the product – remember the EU constitution requiring a referendum which became a revised treaty requiring none? So now, following the government's realisation that the word 'RFID' raised the hackles of the public and got them thinking that, tagged and numbered 'like criminals on parole', they would become subject to onerous surveillance, or as John Lettice so memorably put it, 'crates in the homeland security's supply chain',[6] RFID chips were magically transmuted into 'contactless' or 'proximity' chips. This is why in January 2006 Home Office minister Andy Burnham MP was able to reply to a query from concerned fellow MP Lynne Jones: 'There are no plans to use Radio Frequency Identification tags. They would serve no purpose which is relevant to the identity cards scheme.' So, that's clear. No RFID in the UK's proposed ID cards.

Burnham had given the same response a month earlier, stating that 'there are no plans to use Radio Frequency Identification tags in ID cards'. However, the minister went on to say that suppliers had been 'asked for views on the durability and costs of contact, contactless, dual interface and hybrid cards. This survey concluded that a ten-year life for a *contactless card incorporating a secure smartcard chip with a radio frequency contactless interface* [author's emphasis] was feasible.' Make no mistake, a 'contactless card' with a 'radio frequency contactless interface' is government-speak for an RFID chip.

73

Our biometric passports will contain similar technology. In February 2005 Des Browne, then immigration minister, informed Mark Oaten MP that the 'biometric passport will contain a radio frequency contactless integrated circuit [translation: an RFID chip] that conforms to ISO 14443 in accordance with ICAO recommendations of biometric travel documents. It will be a close proximity chip that can only work within 0–2cm from a reader.' Back at the Home Office, Burnham was making similar pledges on the security of data held in his 'radio frequency chips' (i.e. RFID tags) to be incorporated in the putative ID card: 'We will ensure that sensitive data on the chip is encrypted, and are aiming to do this through adoption of emerging ... ICAO standards. These provide significantly more security of data than exists today.' In addition, Burnham noted that his staff had 'reviewed technical methodologies for anti-skimming measures for contactless cards'. This latter will almost certainly be similar to that proposed for the US biometric passport, which will have a foil barrier built into the cover, preventing the card from being read unless it is opened.

It sounds impressive: encryption of data and 'anti-skimming measures' to prevent illegal reading of the encrypted data that the ID card carries. But, as has been pointed out by several researchers, if the contactless radio frequency device (aka RFID) 'can only work within 0–2 cm from a reader', why do we need anti-skimming measures in the first place?

Because the government is perfectly aware, as several independent tests have shown, that the chips can be read from much greater distances. And once the ID card is in everyone's pocket, we can confidently expect that the identity thieves will be moving heaven and earth to increase that read-range still further, and to hoover up all your priceless, unalterable biometric data, *without your knowledge*, from a nice safe distance.

But then why worry? What use is the data to them? Those clever government boffins have encrypted the data. It can't be read, the information is gobbledegook without the correct key, and the criminal's nefarious schemes will come to naught.

Well, not exactly. Because several individuals have reported that RFID chips' 'collision avoidance system' can act as a channel to undermine any access control. 'They're insecure by design, because the basic design is intended for vast numbers of cheap chips labelling everything in Wal-Mart', says Bruce Schneier in *Wired* magazine.[7] The truth of this statement was made clear in early 2006, when it was shown that the new Dutch biometric passports could be read and their encryption cracked. According to John Lettice of *The Register*,[8] Delft smartcard security specialists Riscure were able to read the card from a distance of 10 metres (compare and contrast with MP Des Browne's '0–2cm'), and the 'secure' card data was cracked in about two hours to reveal date of birth, facial image and fingerprint. Dutch passports are numbered sequentially, which made breaking the encryption faster, but all similar biometric passports and ID cards are vulnerable, 'giving ID thieves and would-be forgers a considerable leg-up in the construction of fakes'.

The Dutch Interior Ministry responded by claiming that work was ongoing to improve the new passport's security. But this misses the point, which is that any breach of the biometric data on an individual's card will compromise that person's security *for life*. As we've seen in chapter 4, biometric data cannot be changed. PINs, cards, even one's signature, are all like keys to a door. Lose one or all of the keys, or have them stolen, and one can quickly change the lock to prevent any unsanctioned access. By contrast, the biometric door has only one immutable lock, and once the key is stolen there is little one can do to prevent unauthorised entry. A fingerprint is uniquely your own, and once someone possesses that fingerprint they can claim your identity wherever fingerprint data is used to confirm identity.

And as several websites have demonstrated, fingerprints can easily be lifted, forged and glued inconspicuously to another's digits. It is clearly not acceptable for the Dutch government to say they are working to 'improve' the system – they, and all other governments contemplating this scheme, need to be sure it is impregnable. Attaching biometric data to a card without being 100 per cent certain it is invulnerable to attack is placing bureaucratic convenience above the interests of the citizen. And since no card is now invulnerable to skimming, nor is it likely to be in the foreseeable future, the conclusion is obvious: biometric data should never be placed on a passport or ID card.

Even without these concerns over superfluous data, illegal card-reading and identity theft, the fact remains that the UK ID card and passport as presently envisaged will still enable the security services, police and various government departments to log your travel, your lifestyle and any transactions where the card must be shown (and these will obviously multiply as the card becomes the gold standard of identity). All data will be accessible, giving a searchable 'Google' of every citizen's life and movements.

And do not even think of refusing to comply. All adult citizens will be required to visit an enrolment centre with sufficient documentation to prove identity (credit cards, driving licence or birth certificate, bank statements; no one is entirely sure what will suffice). You will be fingerprinted and photographed (yes, just like they do on *The Bill* and all the other TV police programmes). Then you must reveal to the authorities 49 specific pieces of information about yourself which they will store in the database along with your biometrics. Failure to attend an 'enrolment interview' will result in a fine of up to £2,500, and another date will be set for your enrolment. Refuse to attend again and you may be fined a further £2,500, and so on, every time you fail to comply.

'There's more. Lose your ID card, and forget to inform the Home Office or police, and there's a fine of up to £1,000. Malfunctioning card, which you omit to mention to the authorities? £1,000. Fail to inform the NIR of any change in address? £1,000. Find another person's card and do not *immediately* hand it in? A criminal offence, punishable by up to two years' imprisonment or a fine. Or both. 'If you don't inform the register of significant changes to your personal life, or any errors they have made, you will face a fine of up to £1,000. Astonishingly, you may also face a fine if you fail to submit to being re-interviewed, re-photographed, re-fingerprinted and rescanned.'[9]

And the worst of it is, it is all unnecessary. Despite UK government ministers' pronouncements, all that is needed to comply with the ICAO standards – which they are so keen to cite as justification for including biometric data on their own passport (and internal ID card) – is a simple digitised passport photograph. *Everything* else is optional. Even the United States government has plumped for just two parameters on that nation's passports: a digitised photograph and fingerprint biometric. By contrast, of the 51 pieces of information that will be held on every individual, New Labour and the Home Office have made provision for the taking of thirteen biometrics – a horrendous and deeply suspicious example of information overkill. The truth is, for the purpose for which the UK government claim they are required, these data are simply not necessary. Which raises the question: why are they being included?

As the ACLU (American Civil Liberties Union) stated at a recent congressional hearing:

RFIDs would allow for convenient, at-a-distance verification of identity. RFID-tagged IDs could be secretly read right through a wallet, pocket, backpack or purse by anyone with the appropriate reader device, including marketers, identity thieves, pickpockets, oppressive governments and others … Pocket ID readers could be used by government agents to sweep up the identities of everyone at a political meeting, protest march, or Islamic prayer service. A network of automated RFID listening posts on the sidewalks and roads could even reveal the location of all people in the US at all times.[10]

If ID cards are made mandatory, with a legal requirement to carry them at all times, there really is nothing to prevent the real-time location of the populations of entire countries being collated in a central database. Already, as we have seen, RFID readers have been experimentally embedded into floor tiles, woven into carpets, hidden in doorways and seamlessly incorporated into retail shelving. Surveillance would be easy, ubiquitous and covert.

6

LOCATION I: The Watchers

What's in a name?

The step-wise, 'stealth' approach we've seen with e-passports and ID cards is one government strategy to ensure gradual acquiescence to the continuing roll-out of surveillance technology. Another is a clear attempt to 'define the topography of the argument', a tactic which has been used with great effect in visual surveillance of the population.

An unrelated example should make this 'topography' concept clearer. Wind turbines are regularly in the news as demonstrators protest against their construction in rural areas of outstanding beauty. Without going into the merits or otherwise of these machines, it must be said that the developers of wind power have already stolen a march on the protestors by succeeding in making the phrase 'wind farm' the generic term for these renewable electricity stations. It's a phrase which even the turbine's detractors are happy to use, thereby immediately, and unconsciously, devaluing their own arguments. Because if what everyone is talking about is a 'wind farm', then where else would one expect to find a 'farm' but in the country?

If we change the name to, say, 'wind factory' (which is probably a much more accurate description for a collection of such huge industrial structures), then the whole perception of the argument changes with it. Many who would be in favour of a 'wind farm' in a beauty spot would think twice about a 'wind factory' in the same location.

Similar examples are everywhere: agribusiness fights against organic farming by naming its own oil-based, insecticide and herbicide-ridden methods 'traditional farming', ignoring the fact that, the last 50 years excepted, organic methods have been the norm ever since humans first broke the earth to plant seed. Educationalists tout 'progressive teaching methods' and immediately gain the high ground of any discussion, for who could be against 'progress' in teaching? If these were given a fairer soubriquet, say 'novel, untried teaching methods', the 'progressives' would immediately be forced back on the defensive: who would risk novel, untried techniques when traditional methods have served us so well in the past?

This same strategy has been noted earlier in the RFID (or as the government would have it, 'contactless' or 'proximity' chip) debate, and we will meet this subterfuge again in following chapters. It has also been used with great effect in visual surveillance. The cameras that watch our every move in urban environments are known, by general consent, as CCTV, the acronym for 'closed circuit television'. The term's association with television makes it unconsciously comforting, because we all know and love the 'telly'. And being 'closed circuit' gives the impression that any images the system captures remain private, or at least restricted to a small number of operators. The fact that CCTV is now no longer either television or closed circuit (see below) does nothing to diminish the power of the name, or the ease with which the technology is accepted by the British public.

If we try the term 'spy camera' instead, the situation changes dramatically. Who in their right mind would be in favour of the blanket coverage of our towns and public spaces by spy cameras? Especially when there are no legal restrictions on the use of these cameras, and such equipment has signally failed to bring about the reduction in crime that was to be our reward, the quid pro quo, for the gross invasion of privacy that is inseparable from the use of such intrusive panoptic surveillance.

While in the process of writing this book, it became obvious that I was missing one crucial example of 'defining the topography of the argument', ignoring a word that, because of its prevalence in this debate and its use by both promoters and detractors, is invisible, yet serves to immediately defuse the anger and concern which should rightfully attach to this topic. So fully had it been hidden in plain sight that I have even used the word in the title of this book, *Surveillance Unlimited*.

Surveillance. A fine neutral word that conveys ideas of a level-headed, objective consideration of the facts surrounding this subject, and serves to sanitise what actually takes place. For what is 'surveillance' but another name for spying? To watch individuals covertly, to film them, to listen in to their communication, to know where they are at any given moment, to amass data on every aspect of their lifestyles – this, surely, is precisely what a spy is paid to do. And this is exactly what our government and large corporations are doing, and attempting to do, to every individual in this nation. I was tempted to use the 'find/exchange' key of my computer to substitute spy-words wherever 'surveillance' had been used in the text, but finally decided against it. Not because a substitution is not valid, but because it is undeniable that surveillance is now so ingrained in the nation's psyche that to try to substitute another word would, as with 'wind farm' and 'CCTV', be doomed to failure. But, as you read these pages, it is worth contemplating a single question: what *is* the difference between 'surveillance' and 'spying'?

Camera capital of the world

Britain has the dubious distinction of leading the world in the deployment of visual surveillance systems. As early as the 1953 coronation of Elizabeth II, a primitive closed circuit television network was used temporarily on the streets of London. But it was the introduction of a video surveillance system at a London train station in 1961 that heralded the arrival of true 'CCTV' on a permanent basis on and below our city streets. At that time image capture was on videotape, and for logistical and space reasons it was not possible to store recorded tracks for much more than two months. Nor were the cassettes easily viewed or transported. All of this militated against a comprehensive, all-seeing surveillance canopy; that was for the future.

Public reaction to this deployment was for the most part favourable throughout the next few decades, and more and more urban areas saw the rollout of increasingly sophisticated CCTV networks, due in part to the popularity of such programmes as *Crimewatch UK* (first screened in 1984), which featured CCTV footage as a prime mover in the fight against crime. In 1985 the Football Trust gave it added impetus when the charity bestowed grants to all football league clubs to help them establish surveillance schemes in their stadiums to fight the increasing incidence of football hooliganism.[1] Again, the rise of the shopping mall throughout the 1980s fuelled the demand for more CCTV. Portrayed in their own advertisements and PR as playgrounds for the people, offering limitless opportunity for 'retail therapy', shopping centres can also be seen as '... places in which users are treated as a means to the ends of consumption, [the owners] employing a number of socially controlling strategies in management, design, promotion and policing to achieve this'.[2] The 'policing' was (and still is) achieved in large part by comprehensive camera surveillance, backed up by security staff who evict loiterers, drunks, beggars, and the homeless – anyone, in fact, who does not serve the needs of the shopping centre's owners by spending money. Such homogenising of the shopping centre's population, this decrease in diversity, has far-reaching effects on societal cohesion (see chapter 13); but such social disadvantages were not even on the political radar during the eighties. The benefits promised by CCTV were immediate: less crime, better security. Few stopped to think about the long-term consequences of establishing an overarching surveillance canopy in our major towns and cities. In fact, as the decade drew to a close, the demand for CCTV systems continued to rise. In August 1994, *Police Review* magazine reported that 'CCTV is now seen as the fashionable solution to everything. Councils are saying we need CCTV, either for political reasons, or because the town next door has got it ...'[3]

Popular approval of CCTV seemed to be based on an almost instinctive belief that the cameras would decrease the level of crime on our streets. It seemed obvious that, if someone was watching – and recording – their behaviour, a criminal would think twice before mugging an old lady, breaking into a house or stealing a car. These impressions were reinforced in the early nineties with the harrowing footage of two-year-old Jamie Bulger being led away by two youths to his untimely death. Such emotion-laden images become etched into the public mind; as Chris Hale has shown, fear of crime is often significantly increased by media images which may involve people or places recognisable to the recipient, for whom the possibility of crime then becomes a reality.[4] Seeing James Bulger's abduction taking place in a shopping centre, an environment familiar to everyone, fed the conviction that such events could happen anywhere, and that something must be done. And despite the fact that the

83

video images neither stopped the awful crime nor identified the youths involved, the idea arose that if only we had had more of these cameras around, this, and similar appalling incidents, might be avoided.

In 1994 the Home Office dispensed £5 million between successful bidders of their 'CCTV Challenge Competition'. Three additional periods of this competition have helped fund the phenomenal expansion of CCTV in the United Kingdom. During the last decade of the 20th century, an astonishing 78 per cent of the Home Office budget for crime reduction was spent setting up CCTV surveillance, with around half a billion pounds invested in CCTV infrastructure. There are now an estimated 4.2 million cameras active on the streets of Britain, one for every fourteen people and 20 per cent of the world's total.[5] City dwellers can expect to be targeted by over 300 cameras each day.[6] Camera surveillance is a growth industry, with an annual spend touching a quarter of a billion pounds.

But does it work?

Despite all this investment, many studies have shown that CCTV has yet to prove it has a cost-effective role in crime reduction. Most of the research suffers from pro-surveillance bias. A research paper in the *Stanford Technology Law Review* concluded that:

> The vast number of evaluation schemes that have been carried out to date have been undertaken by those with an interest in promoting the cameras and have been technically inadequate. Evaluation is often carried out over too short a time for a realistic picture to be gained, and often the full story remains untold. CCTV may ultimately catch more offenders and improve the

crime/clear up ratio, which is important to the police in the era of the audit, but many of these are minor offences which previously may never have been reported at all. A simple look at the crime statistics does not provide a full picture of CCTV's effectiveness and in many cases, over-inflated statistics are simply misleading.[7]

In addition, where studies showed that some degree of crime reduction had been achieved (primarily through CCTV in car parks), almost invariably other measures had been introduced alongside CCTV, making it difficult to determine the efficacy of stand-alone visual surveillance.

Notwithstanding these conclusions, the proponents of CCTV have continued to advertise the 'success' of the technology on the basis of isolated and misleading research. Such narrow-focus triumphalism has failed to take into account an unpalatable fact: in almost all cases where offences were reduced in a given area, the cameras were merely displacing crime, moving it to other, non-surveyed areas. In the late 1980s, Strathclyde police were quick to proclaim a welcome reduction in assaults in the town of Airdrie, down from 171 to 79 in the year following the intro-duction of CCTV surveillance – unfortunately, it was later shown that figures for serious crime across the whole district jumped by 20 per cent over the same period.[8]

The Research, Development and Statistics Directorate of the Home Office, undisputed champion of countrywide CCTV coverage, has been forced to concede that 'the CCTV schemes that have been assessed had little overall effect on crime levels'.

This finding raised other equally serious issues. Knowing that the research evidence showed that CCTV did not work, why was there still such undimmed enthusiasm for the technology, an eagerness that continues unabated today? In our present era of 'value for money', with its almost obsessive concern with target-hitting, why continue to spend billions of pounds on a system that is patently 'not fit for purpose'. Is this a simple example of bureaucratic inertia? Of continuing with a failed policy year after year because there is nothing better to hand, and even if the system is not working, the ever-increasing number of cameras at least gives a trusting public the *impression* that something is being done to curb crime? There appears to be no other reason for going ahead with ever-increasing CCTV coverage, despite compelling evidence that it is not doing the job it was supposed to do – unless, of course, there is another task that the spy cameras are intended to perform. If we remove the supposed rationale for comprehensive CCTV coverage of the vast majority of the population as they go about their daily lives (i.e. CCTV = crime reduction), we are left with a system whose primary function is to watch the citizen. What is needed are clear, legally enforceable rules for the regulation of CCTV.

There is a further problem. Irrespective of its true raison d'être, the creation of such a powerful surveillance system brings great temptation to those who operate it. Studies in the UK have revealed that a significant number of (predominantly male) operators use the cameras to view pretty women. Around 10 per cent of women targeted by these operators were brought under surveillance for purely voyeuristic reasons. Racial stereotypes also skew the gaze of the operators, with 'black people between one-and-a-half and two-and-a-half times more likely to be surveilled than one would expect from the presence in the population'.[9] Of even greater concern is the possibility of institutional abuse. Organised government harassment of dissidents is by no means confined to 'non-democratic' states, especially during times of civil disturbance, international conflict or strenuous protest against government policies. Both anti-Vietnam War protestors and members of the civil rights movement in the USA were victims of illegal surveillance by the FBI. Given that we seem to be experiencing a similar period of controversy today, especially concerning UK foreign policy, it will be an enormous temptation for government departments to use the comprehensive surveillance information provided by CCTV to target even peaceful protest groups.

Compounding this are simple errors, and the stressful ordeal of being wrongly accused on the basis of CCTV evidence. Alexandra Campbell gave a graphic account of her ordeal for alleged credit card theft and deception.[10] The card had been stolen from a health club of which she was a member, and CCTV images revealed an unknown woman shopping with the stolen card nearby. The health club receptionist identified the person on the CCTV footage as Ms Campbell and the police required her to come up to London (she had recently moved out of the capital) for an interview. This demand meant the costly hiring of a lawyer to accompany her to the interview, and resulted in two worry-filled sleepless nights and the loss of two days' work. Despite having been in East Sussex on the day in question, and having her presence there confirmed by her brother and her sister-in-law (both of whom were barristers), she was promptly booked in and questioned on her mental health, the possibility of self-harm and whether she would wish to see a drugs counsellor, and then left alone while the policewoman in charge outlined the evidence to her lawyer in an interview room. Notwithstanding the fact that the police had intimated that they had 'other evidence', and said that her presence was required at the police station so they could 'disclose all the evidence' to her lawyer, after which she could 'discuss how you want to play it', the evidence turned out to be a statement by the woman whose purse had been stolen that the thief was 'about 35 and dark-haired'. Ms Campbell was 50 years old with white-blonde hair.

CCTV surveillance also raises questions of social justice. Not only is it obvious that overall crime remains unaffected by CCTV systems, displacement of crime is seen to disadvantage the least well off in our communities. One feature of present-day CCTV surveillance is that the cameras tend to be sited in high-value commercial areas of our towns and cities. The presence of these cameras deters miscreants from the area, and ejects those prepared to commit offences from the more affluent sections of our cities into low-rent deprived areas, which then experience an unlooked-for increase in crime. This is patently unfair and socially divisive; is it right that those with more means or political clout can pass on their own crime burden to those less able to pay? If the affluent can afford to displace crime to poorer areas, we are fast on our way to one deputy police commissioner's depressing image of 'crime free enclaves protected by the best that money can buy, yet surrounded by a sea of criminality'.[11]

In addition, the fixation of the authorities on CCTV coverage has undermined (and removed resources from) other more traditional approaches to law enforcement that carry far fewer risks to civil liberties. In 1992, Exeter City Council scrapped a planned CCTV system and used the funds saved to employ six extra policemen. By contrast, the residents of Bingley near Bradford saw CCTV installed, and witnessed an almost immediate reduction of police numbers in their area – from an original 24 officers down to just three. Many towns no longer have a routine police presence at their nightclub and drinking areas in the late evening and at 'closing time'. While an officer on the beat has a far better feel for any situation that may be developing, and can intervene in good time and perhaps reason with those on the point of causing a disturbance, the preferred strategy now is to watch and wait for signs of trouble via CCTV (while at the same time checking on, recording and logging the behaviour and movement of every law-abiding citizen within range of the cameras).

There is an even more insidious aspect to the multitude of cameras that now plague our environment. The constant visual surveillance to which we are subjected can only habituate us to other surveillance technologies. If our every move is already monitored, recorded and logged by camera, why should we worry about fingerprinting of children, DNA banks, remotely-readable RFID passports or mandatory ID cards? The more cameras we are exposed to, the easier it becomes to persuade us to take the next step along the road to total control.

Faced with these facts, public approval of CCTV surveillance has fallen significantly from the mid-nineties onwards. Another reason for dissatisfaction is the belated interest now being taken in the threats to civil liberties, anonymity and privacy that CCTV surveillance brings. These questions were brought sharply into focus in mid-1995 by an unlikely civil liberties hero, the former deputy commissioner of the Metropolitan Police, Sir John Smith. At an IBM seminar entitled *Citizen and State*, Sir John voiced the then-unfashionable opinion that Britain was in danger of becoming an Orwellian society where every citizen lived under constant surveillance. The ex-policeman's concern was that such gross intrusion into people's affairs would foster distrust in both government and the bureaucracy, and distance the citizen from the state.

Sir John's comments were given a good degree of media coverage, but it was the release of a commercial video, *Caught in the Act*, later that same year that really caught public attention. The programme showed an armed robbery, various assaults, drug use, graffiti, shoplifting, car theft, parking fee evasion and footage of a couple making love in a lift. This latter sequence caused public outrage – not for the decline in national morality, but because the intimate shots suddenly brought home to the British population the level of scrutiny to which they were already subjected. (Ironically, the love-making sequence was later found to have been staged. However, according to CCTV operators I have spoken with, such scenes are far from uncommon in the pageant of life that regularly passes across their screens.) The media took up the story, and readers and viewers were soon regaled with tales of hidden cameras on public transport, inside toilets, changing rooms and telephone booths, and in police cars and automatic teller machines. The public was 'brought face to face with the reality, rather than the ideal, of CCTV. The film highlighted the extent to which CCTV could be used as a means of enforcing public morality and public order.'[12]

The growing presence of the all-seeing eye of CCTV can only bring about subtle but profound changes to the character of our public spaces. People deemed to be 'out of place' in an area are already subjected to prolonged surveillance. Increasing video scrutiny will have a chilling effect on public life. American columnist Jacob Sullum has stated the problem clearly: 'Knowing that you are being watched by armed government agents tends to put a damper on things. You don't want to offend them or otherwise call attention to yourself ... people may learn to be careful about the books and periodicals they read in public, avoiding titles that might alarm unseen observers. They may also put more thought into how they dress, lest they look like terrorists, gang members, druggies or hookers.' Far from being the nation of free-wheeling risk-takers that have helped make Britain one of the foremost economies in the world, CCTV could well turn the UK into a population of risk-averse conformists.

There have been periodic outcries against visual surveillance ever since Sir John's pioneering attack on CCTV networks, but such protests have in no way affected government funding for, and the deployment of, an ever-increasing number of spy cameras across the urban landscape. The latest analysis of the dangers of this strategy, part of the Royal Academy of Engineering's 2007 report *Dilemmas of Privacy and Surveillance*, identifies three main aspects of video surveillance which are responsible for a raft of political, social and technical problems.

First, it is citizens in public spaces who are the objects of surveillance. This threatens to destroy the 'public privacy' previously enjoyed by anonymous citizens in a public space.

Second, citizens are in no position to agree to or reject surveillance. This limits the extent of the freedom of citizens to go about their lawful business without being observed and monitored. It also extends the capacity for agencies and institutions to subject a section of the public realm to surveillance for their own purposes.

Third, the development of surveillance systems has changed what can be gleaned from observations of individuals. As well as recording the presence of and recognising individuals, surveillance systems now offer the possibility of evaluating and making inferences about a person's actions and intentions, drawing on stereotypes and profiling methods.

Seeing further, seeing more

CCTV is now a misleading title. In the early days of the technology, images were captured on tape and access by, say, the police required that they visit the CCTV operations centre, or that the tapes be physically transported to the police station. This, along with the necessity of wiping the tapes every eight weeks or so owing to storage problems, and the fact that each tape needed to be scanned visually by a human operator, served to limit the usefulness of the system and kept the technology within reasonable bounds.

None of these limitations apply today, and the term CCTV

is now a misnomer. As the RAE report mentioned above points out: 'Modern surveillance systems are no longer "closed-circuit", and increasing numbers of surveillance systems use networked, digital cameras rather than CCTV. The continued use of the term is an indicator of a general lack of awareness of the nature of contemporary surveillance, and disguises the kinds of purposes, dangers and possibilities of current technologies.'

The report says that these new visual surveillance systems should be known as 'public webcams', as 'they can be – and often are – linked as a network covering a wide space; their footage can be streamed to the internet or TV; the footage is stored digitally and it can be searched using image searching technologies. These webcams are public in that they capture images from public spaces, including images of members of the public. They change private or anonymous behaviour into publicly available images, and they can potentially transmit for public consumption anything captured digitally.'

The RAE's concern over new video surveillance technologies is well founded. The data bandwidth and data requirements are truly gigantic – just a single frame at full resolution needs around 676 KB of memory. At the standard viewing rate of 30 frames per second, each second of footage requires 20.3 MB, or around a gigabyte per minute. Such demands would fill a 40 GB hard drive in around three-quarters of an hour, and at first glance could not possibly be a practical or affordable solution to video surveillance. But thanks to digital compression techniques, and increases in computer memory and software, the video signal can now be handled with ease. Compressed digital video is readily stored and transported on a variety of media, making remote surveillance and automatic archiving possible. Such flexibility has given contemporary visual surveillance a truly Olympian capacity to scrutinise our lives. CCTV systems are often compared to the work of an ever-vigilant police officer, but increasing sophistication and technological advances have made the visual surveillance networks we now face on a daily basis far more than just a simple substitute for the bobby on the beat.

Camera capability

Modern cameras are quasi-military equipment, direct descendants of the military surveillance systems pioneered at such defence centres as the Faslane nuclear submarine base. As there, the cameras are set out in networks so that each unit can be viewed by at least one other camera, enabling any attempt at sabotage by members of the public (and such sabotage remains a vastly under-reported story) to be detected, and evidence of the incident filmed. Many cameras have now been enclosed in transparent bullet-proof casings. The capabilities of even the most basic models are frightening: high quality, full-colour digital images are the norm, with cameras that can pan and tilt, and lenses that can zoom in from 250 metres to read the fine print of your newspaper. The cameras can operate in total darkness, using infra-red and computer buffering to prevent glare from headlights and street lamps obscuring the image of whatever event or person is under scrutiny. Recently, there was the inevitable outcry when high-powered parabolic microphones were mooted for the London 2012 Olympics, so that camera operators could not only see, but hear, everything that occurs within their range, day or night. The microphones can pick up conversations 100 yards away, and detect aggressive tones on the basis of twelve factors, including decibel level, pitch and the speed at which words are spoken. Completing the compelling Big Brother parallels, the authorities in Darlington, County Durham have recently piloted 'shouting CCTV', with loudspeakers attached to various positions throughout the town, allowing operatives to admonish miscreants verbally while themselves remaining anonymous.

As one might expect, such arbitrary assignment of guilt has led to a number of mistakes, with law-abiding citizens suddenly verbally assaulted from loudspeakers by nameless accusers for acts they have not committed – and with no possibility of explaining themselves. Shouting CCTV systems have been deployed in several cities, including London, Birmingham and Glasgow, with a fanfare of publicity and high hopes for their role in crime prevention. Unfortunately, while ordinary folk undoubtedly find the apparatus intimidating, no one seems to have considered the fact that toughened law-breakers by definition break the law, and are unlikely to cease their nefarious activities because of a loud voice. This was emphasised in Wakefield in June 2004, when thieves broke into a modern business park which with delicious irony was home to HM Inspectorate of Constabulary and HM Prison Service, and snaffled 60 'shouting cameras', despite repeated admonishments from the loudspeakers to stop. In a touching display of confidence in his newly-nicked system, director Simon Houlston told the *Daily Telegraph*: 'This was a seriously sophisticated system. There are cameras hooked up to a central office in Blackburn. If the men watching the screens see a burglar they send a message out on loudspeakers to the office warning them to leave.' Fabulous technology, but of little use if the raider continues to filch regardless. The biggest effect of the repeated admonishments was to convince an old lady living nearby that she was hearing the voice of God 'telling her, in a strong Lancashire accent, to leave the vicinity as soon as possible'.[13]

Software and analysis

Automatic face recognition (AFR) is a key area of research and development in CCTV systems. AFR normally relies on capturing images using either ambient or infra-red light, a mixture of both or (much more rarely) using stereoscopic systems. The resulting photograph is then compared against a set of standardised face ingredients called 'eigenfaces'. All human faces can be considered as being made up of varying proportions of these eigenfaces, and the facial photograph under study is assigned a series of values from the eigenface set: for example, 'eigenface 1 – 22 per cent; eigenface 2 – 5 per cent; eigenface 3 – 17 per cent', and so on until the complete face has been tabulated. Strangely, it does not take many eigenfaces to produce a reasonable likeness of any face. We should note, too, that the face is no longer recorded as a digital photograph, but simply as a series of numbers, one for each eigenface. This has unfortunate parallels with fingerprints that 'are not fingerprints, just numbers', and we should perhaps be prepared for future attempts to digitise school photographs using the same lame excuse.

AFR technology has been around for some time, most notoriously in the 'Snooperbowl' fiasco of 2001, when Tampa police secretly face-scanned 100,000 fans as they entered the stadium in an attempt to locate known criminals. The test itself was a fiasco, as the nineteen 'hits' generated by the 'Visage' software used were never checked to determine if they had indeed identified a miscreant, but the high-handed invasion of privacy and anonymity of so many people at a single event created a furore, and gave warning for future mass surveillance attempts. Both CCTV and facial recognition software systems have advanced since that time thanks to a huge number of research projects, such as the work done under the auspices of the DTI by Dr Tim Cootes at the University of

Manchester on 'developing systems to link facial biometrics with vehicle identification technologies to support authentication in "drive-in" retail applications'.[14]

At present, recognition performance is susceptible to changes in both light and the position of the person photographed relative to the camera, because differences in lighting can produce greater apparent alteration in a single human face than the differences seen between the faces of different individuals. Intriguingly, the relatively high incidence of twins in the population can also limit the efficiency of the systems. Facial recognition algorithms are presently restricted to full-face shots of an individual in reasonable lighting conditions; this is one reason why most new traffic cameras are sited so that they point at the oncoming traffic and can capture not just traffic movement and registration numbers, but facial features too. 'Full frontal' photography is not always possible in some surveillance situations, and several companies have been experimenting with systems to persuade those 'targeted' to pose as required. The simplest and probably most effective to date is probably 'Sound Alert Technology', where an intruder triggers a hidden switch which in turn fires a short pulse of directional broadband sound, causing the subject to look towards the source of that sound, a loudspeaker sited next to the camera. This permits a full facial shot to be captured; the trigger can be activated either manually (remotely) or automatically (by tripping an infra-red or other beam), or alternatively it can be software-driven.

Once captured, the digital image may be sent anywhere in the world and compared to any other photograph in a given database. This was not perhaps of any great concern when the only searchable photographs on file were those of terrorists and criminals who featured in the rogues' galleries of various police and security agencies. But with the introduction of the digitised passport photo, and the similar image proposed for the new ID card, the balance of power between state and citizen has dramatically changed. Since the end of the last millennium, around 3.5 million images have been added to the database each year, together with personal and family details. At the time of writing, it is estimated that the Identity and Passport Service has a searchable archive of around 47 million people, more than three-quarters of the entire population of the UK. ID card regulations will mean that soon every adult face in the country will be on a central database. Despite Home Office assurances that the system would be operated in strict accordance with the Data Protection Act, the assistant data protection registrar said his office had not been consulted 'formally or informally about this', and that the project was 'in a different league'. We will, it seems, have very little comeback when our privacy is invaded and our anonymity in public spaces compromised, assuming that we are even aware that such violations have taken place.

The Home Office claim that the new database is a necessary step to combat passport fraud was given short shrift by Simon Davies of Privacy International: 'It's always been the wet dream of authority to link faces with data and this will be a red letter day for them. The fraud argument is a confidence trick, as the new passports will be just as easy to forge. The only winners will be the police, security services and anybody else – except of course ordinary people.'[15]

Possibly the least intrusive of all surveillance attempts at identification at a distance is gait recognition. Essentially, this attempts to identify a specific individual by the way they walk. This is not as easy as it might first appear, especially in normal urban situations, but great advances have been made in the past few years.[16] Researchers have devised 'background subtraction algorithms' to isolate the subject under surveillance from the confusing 'noise' of their surroundings, to silhouette the subject for ease of calculation, and to track the moving silhouette. An 'eigenspace transformation' (similar to the 'eigenface' used in facial recognition) gives a specific value to various features of that person's gait. The sum of these values gives a specific identity, which is claimed to be as unique as a fingerprint.

Link this information to a database of names, addresses, ages and whatever else has been garnered from other bureaucratic additions and voilà! Public anonymity has vanished. Provided you are on foot, a gait-enabled camera can pick you out in seconds from any crowded street. And all without you being aware that you are an object of scrutiny.

The Royal Society has now gone one stage further, and has recently joined forces with the National Science Foundation of China (NSFC) to fund a project to develop models for the fusion of multiple biometrics (human face recognition and gait), so that any errors generated by one system will be compensated for by the other. Leaving aside the question of the wisdom of the Royal Society cooperating with a regime which is not renowned for its human rights record, the aim of the project remains chillingly clear: 'This joint project will investigate novel algorithms to combine facial image identification with both typical and abnormal human action and gait patterns *in order to perform non-intrusive person identification from a distance in public space CCTV data*' [author's emphasis]. Furthermore, the nature of this research serves to emphasise the power to be had from an amalgamation of a whole series of identity technologies, an aim which digitisation and networking has made simple.

Networks

Unlike videotape, digital recording allows for the storage of an almost infinite number of images; such recordings can be played back and duplicated repeatedly without quality degradation. Viewing the images is also easier; digital access is immediate, so no more time wasted in winding down to the required sequence.

All these advantages are given added impetus when systems and databases are networked, via either landline or the internet. Broadband, along with other advances in computer-to-computer communication, means that a camera net can offer total surveillance of any given area, with images made available in real time to anyone with the reception capability, anywhere in the world. Add this to facial recognition software linked to a police or other government database (e.g. the Identity and Passport Service, or the National Identity Register) and we are all in danger of losing our public anonymity. Any CCTV operative can know within seconds who you are, and bring up a vast range of personal details.

ANPR and EVI

And the problem is set to get worse. The Association of British Drivers, in backing a 'stop road pricing' petition, has pointed to the civil liberties dimension of the scheme, stating that 'Britain's drivers will be targeted 24 hours a day, seven days a week by a spy network comprising satellites, ANPR (Automatic Number Plate Recognition) cameras, and roadside tracking devices. Privacy will become a thing of the past.' The government, in the form of former transport minister Douglas Alexander, has responded by claiming that there will be 'safeguards' to deal with privacy. We have to be very careful here, and for two reasons: first, the government has already denied that the scheme threatens privacy; if they continue to hold to this position, then logically 'safeguards' to protect privacy would not, in their view, be necessary.

Why bother to bring in legislation for a non-existent problem? Second, as with all such assurances, there will be the habitual exemption for law enforcement and the security services. No matter how many 'safeguards' pass into law, the state will still be able to circumvent these restrictions for 'security reasons' and monitor all Britain's drivers on a constant, hour-by-hour basis.

Despite government denials, the police themselves are mustard-keen on the technology and not afraid to show it. The Association of Chief Police Officers' (ACPO) March 2005 paper *Denying Criminals the Use of the Roads* shows that the ACPO is eager to establish 'a national ANPR camera and reader infrastructure utilising police, local authority, Highways Agency and other partner and commercial sector cameras' in order to exploit 'the full potential of ANPR'. It is clear from this that the police are seeking to establish ANPR function in all cameras, and to link these in a common network. We have already seen this policy in action with the connecting of garage forecourt cameras to the police net. *Denying Criminals the Use of the Roads* talks this proposal up with its slogan 'Think crime, think car, think ANPR' and by imagining the benefits such surveillance will bring in a fictional town of Sandford. Chief Superintendent 'Jones' tells us:

> We recently linked into the ANPR system over 40 of our garage forecourts. They benefit from our intelligence telling them which vehicles to take payment from before they serve them. In return, we get a considerable reduction in forecourt crime, more intelligence on vehicle movements and confirmation of the identities of those using the cars ... We now have a very full picture of which vehicles move, when and where.[17]

Let us be clear. Right now, in garage forecourts all over the UK, each time you pull in for petrol your image is transmitted to the police, who identify you and your car, and bring up any 'relevant' information they need about you. This is not simply about 'Sandford' or any individual town in the United Kingdom. And what is being proposed (all in the name of helping the public) is blanket surveillance of every vehicle on our roads 'and confirmation of the identities of those using the cars', via an enormous network using virtually every CCTV camera in the country that covers any strip of road. Vehicle and driver movement records for any given time or area, all at the drop of a keystroke. A database which is, additionally, linked to other mega-databases so that most aspects of a driver's life can be brought on-screen in a matter of seconds.

This linking of visual imagery to enormous databases containing a vast array of personal details is just one aspect of the hugely intrusive and seemingly unstoppable trend towards total 'dataveillance' that we will be looking at in chapter 10. The problem for opponents of the spy cameras, as with many other forms of surveillance, is that the legal controls have lagged far behind technological advances.

Few legal constraints

Although article 12 of the UN Universal Declaration of Human Rights and article 8 of the European Convention on Human Rights give some notional protection (see chapter 12), there are virtually no legal constraints on the use of visual surveillance systems, and the government seems to have preferred it that way right from the start. In 1993, following Birmingham City Council's suspension of a CCTV planning application, the law was changed to exempt such systems from planning consent. The Tory government constantly reiterated its opposition to legislation, but work by the Local Government Information Unit resulted in a voluntary code which had been adopted by most councils by the time of the 1997 Labour election victory. Labour's attitude to legislation has mirrored that of the Tories, with the London Borough of Brent's May 2007 document *CCTV Strategy* making no mention of legal restrictions and stating only that 'CCTV operations will be carried out fairly and comply with any relevant national and local Codes of Practice' (paragraph 5.1). It remains true that anyone can set up a surveillance network. No real limits have been placed on the purpose for which they are used, nor is there any restraint on the sort of technology that can be added. The irony is that a lone photographer must obtain a signed 'model release' form from anyone he photographs before using a still photograph of his subject(s), yet CCTV captures continuous moving images of thousands of people each day, sends them over networks, subjects them to detailed intrusive analysis, and stores them indefinitely, with never a sign of a legal waiver from any of its unwilling subjects.

Given the extent and intensity of scrutiny we are all exposed to on a daily basis, there is an obvious and urgent need for legally enforceable rules to establish operational parameters for visual surveillance systems. Legal constraints on when and where it is permissible to record images of individuals, on the length of time they are retained, who is to be allowed access to archived footage and on what basis, must all be spelled out. In addition, legislation detailing how these rules will be verified and enforced must also be passed. Finally, there should be severe legal sanctions available (including custodial sentences) for any individual or company who attempts to violate this legal ring-fence around our right to privacy.

Before this can happen there must be a national debate to establish consensus on what limits we wish to impose on visual surveillance systems. All technology tends to expand and converge, revealing new methods of using existing components. CCTV is a prime example of this 'function creep'. We have gone from true 'closed circuit' systems comprising a dozen or so cameras recording on bulky cassettes to huge networks of digital video surveillance, networked to databases of mind-blowing capacity and complexity, from manually-operated cameras to algorithm-run independent units capable of noticing, and zooming in on, 'anomalous behaviour', from cameras that operated only in daylight to machines with infra-red night vision, and with the capacity to see beneath clothing and through walls. The functional concept behind CCTV has crept from simple human surveillance of specific streets and neighbourhoods to prevent crime and vandalism, to systems that pry into every aspect of our lives and destroy public anonymity, the hard-won right to go about your own legal business without the threat of your every action being watched, recorded and analysed, your identity established by facial features or gait. The all-seeing eye now records and logs aspects of our daily life never conceived of when the technology was first deployed just a few short decades ago: everything from recording and logging the registration numbers of all cars using our motorways and watching us at work, to observing our movements on buses, trains and planes, via fixed post systems, mini-cams, police head-cams at ground level and silent helicopter drones above our heads. CCTV function has not so much crept as raced ahead of any national discussion on the acceptability or otherwise of its multifarious roles. Lack of debate has already led to the present parlous state of visual and other privacy issues; we are not in danger of becoming a surveillance state, because we have already arrived. By refusing to debate the issue fully, by relying on pious promises and toothless 'voluntary codes', we are compounding the problem, allowing more and more of our traditional freedoms to fall beneath the wheels of an all-but-unstoppable surveillance juggernaut.

Visual surveillance does not come only from overtly-mounted CCTV cameras; a host of new devices have recently increased authority's capacity for intrusive observation of our private lives. Hidden mini-cams can now be found just about every-where: on buses, in stations and tube trains, in telephone booths, public toilets, cinemas and shops, at ATMs. Passive Millimetre Wave Imagers, essentially cameras which can see under your clothes, are now being trialled at specific stations around London. According to the press release, it will be 'the first use on the UK railway of body scanners using millimetre wave technology. This enables security staff to check for objects concealed under clothing. The trial will test the usefulness of the specialist equipment and help examine the practical issues that may affect its future use in a normal rail environment.' It seems that, very soon, the only time one is likely to be 'safe' from visual surveillance is when one is closeted behind the walls of one's own home.

But, in fact, not even there. Mobile Forward Looking Infra Red (FLIR) units can detect very slight temperature differen-tials and produce a reasonable image of 'hidden' individuals, and an even more sensitive device has recently been deployed by US forces in Iraq. The handheld 'Radar Scope' developed by the US Defense Advanced Research Projects Agency (DARPA) has the ability to tell within seconds if someone is in the next room. By simply holding the portable, handheld device up to a wall, users are able to sense through a foot of concrete and 50 feet into the room beyond, to detect movements as small as breathing.

According to Edward Baranoski of DARPA's Special Projects Office, the organisation is already planning even more advanced systems. New 'Visi Building' technology will actually 'see' through multiple walls, penetrating entire buildings to show floor plans, locations of occupants and placement of materiel.

'It will give [troops] a lot of opportunity to stake out buildings and really see inside', said Baronoski. 'It will go a long way in extending their surveillance capabilities.'[18]

Given the way in which military surveillance technology has invariably migrated to police and other 'law and order' departments of civilian life, we can confidently expect to see this new addition to the surveillance net on our streets within the next several years. Such devices will likely be coupled with microwave sound recording technology, to allow police and other government departments to see and hear everything that occurs within any building.

Of course, for CCTV and other visual surveillance to work, one has to be within visual or auditory range of the equipment. Unfortunately, new advances in the field of remote sensing means that this annoying constraint is no longer a limiting factor.

7

LOCATION II: TOWARDS
A MARAUDER'S MAP

In the third book of the *Harry Potter* series, teenage wizard Harry discovers a magic parchment, the 'Marauder's Map', upon which it is possible to watch the movements of every person present at Hogwarts wizarding school. Possession of the map confers a great deal of power on the student wizard; with its aid he is able to find his friends and, perhaps more importantly, observe his enemies, using the map to escape the attentions of those that may wish him ill, to spy upon their actions and use this knowledge to further his own goals. We may not believe in magic, but new technology, already implemented or in development, will give government its own electronic Marauder's Map, capable of locating its citizens with an astonishing degree of accuracy, and surveying their activities at any given time.

Credit card surveillance

A close friend of mine was shocked to discover the ease with which credit cards can be used to track an individual. Three years ago, while attending a wedding party in Scotland, he was present when one of the guests was given the distressing news that her father had died, entirely unexpectedly, at his home in

England. She was naturally upset, and desperate to get the information to her brother as soon as possible. Unfortunately, he was not at his usual address, but on an overnight trip to London. All she knew of her sibling's whereabouts was that he was in London. Distracted with worry, she was approached by another guest who offered his help: he had a friend who worked at GCHQ, and was sure that this friend would lend his assistance in this emergency. He required her brother's name and address – nothing else. With these provided, the Good Samaritan made a phone call south of the border, obtained a promise of help, and within ten minutes the 'target's' credit card numbers (and perhaps much else) were accessed. Half an hour later, a phone call stated that the lady's brother had bought X amount of petrol at a service station on Park Lane. Just over an hour later, another call informed her that her brother had purchased a room at a certain hotel, and gave the establishment's contact phone number and the 'target's' room number.

That such information can be extracted so easily must be a cause for concern. Given the power of the GCHQ computer base, what can be done for one individual can likely be done, without their knowledge or consent, to tens of thousands of British citizens at any one time. Oyster cards, smart cards and the like pose similar dangers. Each transaction you make is linked to the card you use and logged in the card's central database. Wherever you go – on public transport, in shops, or on the road – you will leave a 'transaction trail' that can be followed by anyone who has the know-how or motivation to track you. Should the European Union carry out their proposal to put RFID chips in paper money, then the final means of conducting business transactions anonymously will have disappeared.

If the banking fraternity have their way, money itself will soon reach the end of its shelf-life. Cash, we are told, is a most inefficient system of exchange. Cash is dirty; cash is heavy

(£1 million in £20 bills weighs much more than most people can lift); cash is expensive to print, transport, hold secure, and count. Cash, in short, is obsolete.

The next big thing is electronic money: Mondex, Bitbux, E-Cash, Netchex, CyberCash, Netbills, DigiCash and a host of other hopefuls. Digital money is perfect money, weighing nothing and moving about the globe at the speed of light. It is networked money, money on a credit card, and money on a computer, transformed at last from bullion and notes to pure information. 'Money is the current liability of a bank,' says Sholom Rosen, electronic cash expert at Citibank. 'It's as simple as that: it's not gold, it's not silver, it's the current liability of a bank.'[1] Large amounts of money are already sent digitally bank to bank; so why not extend this ability to the man in the street, helping to prevent (say its proponents) robbery, bribery, kidnapping, fraud and tax evasion?

The short answer to this is because digital money is digitised money – every transaction recorded and stored on one or more databases, in corporate or government hands. If we accept the demise of cash and its replacement with e-cash, then we are buying into a world where vast databases track your every transaction: each newspaper or magazine you buy, every train, plane or bus you ride, every hamburger, beer or bottle of wine you consume, your supermarket purchases, every video you rent, every book you borrow or buy. And because the location of each purchase is also recorded, anyone with access to the data will know where you have been and what you have done. Everything recorded, stored, analysed and profiled. Private detectives will lose their livelihood – no gumshoe with camera and notebook could hope to amass one tenth of the information that e-cash audit trails will provide about an individual's life and lifestyle. Once e-cash is ubiquitous, there will be very little that the state, or those prepared to pay, will not know about a nation's citizens.

Nor will this data remain passive: information is a valuable commodity. Even in the absence of the comprehensive life-audit that electronic money can provide, numerous facets of our daily life and movement remain open to scrutiny and sale. Right now, the spending details of hundreds of thousands of individuals are obtained via credit and debit cards, loyalty cards etc, and are sold on to the marketing departments of numerous businesses. Collating these various surveillance aspects is now a relatively simple matter, and allows an alternative method for compiling an intimate life-log of any individual.

Charge it to my mobile

Recent developments mean that mobile phones could soon become the method of choice for making payments in e-money. According to electronics website Digital Trends, Japanese mobile phone operator NTT DoCoMo is marketing the i-mode FeliCa handset to act as an electronic wallet: 'An i-mode FeliCa user will be able to wave the handset over a sensor to pay transit fares, buy goods or confirm his or her personal identity to gain access to a location. The i-mode FeliCa will allow users to buy from the 9,000 outlets participating in Sony's Edy e-money system. DoCoMo's system brings together the worlds of prepaid and postpaid transactions.'[2] Convenient? Yes. But, as always, the electronic transfer of money leaves a transaction trail that can and will be recorded, stored and passed on to who knows how many databases. Once again, your activity and your location are open to scrutiny.

But eschewing the joys of e-transactions on your mobile will not keep your location hidden – simply carrying a cellphone in your pocket is equivalent to carrying a radio transmitter saying 'here I am' wherever you go. As we'll see in chapter 8, the content of mobile phone 'traffic' is far from secure, but as well as listening in to conversations, the mobile signal itself can be used to triangulate your position using the nearest mobile masts to within a few metres. Of course, if you have a GPS-enabled phone, some networks can locate you with an accuracy of less than 10 metres. Even when you're not using your mobile, as long as the device is turned on, the phone periodically sends a 'here I am' signal, or 'ping', to phone masts as you move from area to area, and these too can be triangulated.[3] For example, the Vodafone network is said to 'store the Last Known Location, i.e. the Cell ID (and time/date) which the phone was connected to last when switched off, or at least the one to which it was connected during the last automatic "best signal strength" check which occurs every six to ten minutes even if no calls are being made or received ...' There is nothing sinister in this. Knowing just where the phone is located helps the network to decide how best to connect your calls. But, of course, each 'ping' also reveals your location to any interested party who might be listening.

Several companies have cashed in on this fact and now offer services to locate any given mobile phone, provided it is within reach of a mobile telephone mast. It's possible to check at random, or you can order 'snail trails', a scheduled determination of location every hour or so, with a report submitted by the company for your analysis. The information can be quite detailed. As one company's website rather tellingly puts it: 'In essence, we get the same data as the police regarding the movement and location of mobiles.'[4]

The service is intended for benign purposes: to aid businesses in keeping track of their employees during work hours, to help parents keep tabs on their children's location, even to aid the location of missing persons. Unfortunately, the flip side of the technology reveals a host of problems: a business may not confine its scrutiny of employees to work hours only; paedophiles may use the system to track potential victims; a suspicious husband or wife could use the service to check on an erring spouse. In an attempt to stop such abuses, yet another 'voluntary code of conduct' has been published, this time by the Mobile Broadband Group, which phone networks in the UK are asking location providers to follow (note that, as with all voluntary codes, implementing its strictures is a request, not a legal requirement).

An important stipulation of the code is that, once a phone is registered as a tracking device, the location companies should send texts at random intervals alerting the phone's owner that they can now be tracked and allowing them to cancel the facility. Unfortunately, a BBC investigation showed that follow-up reminder texts were taking up to two days to be sent. In addition, although the code requires location services to satisfy themselves that both the watcher and the 'watchee' are consenting adults, the same investigation revealed that at least two location services were not asking for proof of age from the person being tracked. Following these revelations the code's regulations have been tightened; but the dangers inherent in the lack of any legislation or sanctions on those flouting the 'voluntary code' are too obvious to labour.

Other intrusive commercial applications are being developed for the technology, such as using location information to send targeted advertisements in the form of text messages to customers. For example, if your mobile locates you at a certain position on the local high street, a multitude of text messages detailing special offers for shops at that location would follow within seconds.

But of course, in this particular case evading both the surveillance web and those annoying text-ads is child's play. As many people are now aware, if you don't want anyone to know where you are, simply switch off your mobile and you'll be invisible (give or take a CCTV camera, credit card transaction, RFID tag or Oyster card). Right? Well, no. Because it seems that at least some mobiles 'ping' whether you want them to or not. Freelance consultant Ben Laurie had experience of one such device and cautions that switching off is no guarantee of invisibility. 'Actually, you need to take the batteries out. My previous mobile (a Nokia 2100) audibly interfered with land lines (or perhaps my headset), and I have caught it registering itself when it is nominally off.'[5]

Nor are the phones that don't 'secretly' ping your location (assuming they exist) totally location-proof. Not, at least, to government agencies. That, in certain circumstances, the authorities can unilaterally switch on your mobile seems confirmed by the account, in *Times* journalist Michael Smith's authoritative book, *Killer Elite*, of the 2002 assassination of an Al Qaeda officer in Yemen:

> There was little doubt that a Toyota Land Cruiser that could be seen ... on the screens at CIA headquarters contained Qa'ed Sunyan al-Harethi, Bin Laden's personal representative in Yemen ... Harethi's mobile phone was being tracked by [US special-forces technicians]. They had been waiting for the moment *when they could remotely programme it to switch itself on*, to provide a target for an attack [author's emphasis].[6]

But mobile phone technology is not limited to eavesdropping on conversations and obtaining location data on individual handsets. Celldar, funded by the British government, uses mobile phone masts to watch individuals and traffic in real time almost anywhere in the UK. The system operates in the same way as radar, using the waves reflected back from mast transmissions to build up a picture of the environment around the mast. Software filters out all objects such as walls or trees, allowing moving objects, such as vehicles or people, to be tracked. The system is intended for remote viewing of any part of the country with a mobile phone mast, and a portable unit has been developed to act as a personal radar around the operator. 'Researchers are working to give the new equipment "X-ray vision" – the capability to "see" through walls and look into people's homes … The researchers themselves say the system … is aimed at anti-terrorism defence, security and traffic management.'[7]

It's not as if our car journeys aren't already subject to surveillance. CCTV aside, all main arteries inside the M25 are fitted with cameras equipped with OCR (optical character recognition) software, allowing the police to know within minutes just whose car is travelling into and out of the capital. A 24/7/365 national vehicle movement database that logs everything on the UK's roads and retains the data for at least two years is in the process of being rolled out, according to an Association of Chief Police Officers (ACPO) spokesman. The system uses Automatic Number Plate Recognition (ANPR), and will be overseen from a control centre in Hendon, London, extending, enhancing and linking existing CCTV, ANPR and speed camera systems and databases. The control centre is designed to process over 50 million number plates a day. According to ACPO roads policing head Meredydd Hughes, ANPR systems are planned every 400 yards along motorways. The deployment of what promises to be one the most pervasive surveillance systems on earth went ahead without needing any parliamentary approval.

Road toll cards allow similar, though less comprehensive, monitoring of car movement. Satellite surveillance of car journeys is now being mooted by the government as the easiest way to monitor and charge for the new toll roads being proposed in the UK. The civil liberties implications of this technology are enormous. That the government can quietly watch the car journeys of all individuals with such ease must be cause for concern.

Were every motorway bridge to be garrisoned with police observers monitoring our every car journey, we would be rightly outraged at the infringement on our liberties. Yet when the same procedure occurs remotely, from space, it appears to pass without comment. When one considers that other European countries plan (or have already implemented) similar strategies, it is obvious that movement across entire continents will soon be routinely monitored. The 'freedom of the open road' will be no more than an illusion.

Identity check

While they remain deeply worrying, the technologies of the preceding paragraphs are thankfully not foolproof; one may have lent a friend one's car, or mobile phone, and those interested in a specific 'target's' movements may end up following an electronic wild goose chase without ever realising their mistake. But as we've seen in chapter 4, technology firms have risen to this challenge, and are now deploying systems that will automatically check personnel files and recognise an individual face from hundreds of thousands of others.

American-designed software 'Combat Zones That See' (CTS) is attempting to put all these many facets together in a single device that can provide detailed surveillance in urban areas. The necessity of US forces engaging 'asymmetrical forces' (guerrillas and insurgents) in sustained street fighting has become increasingly clear over the past few years. Such urban areas are three-dimensional, with large buildings, extensive underground passageways and concealment from above, making traditional 'standoff' surveillance via airborne and satellite imagery ineffective. The short lines of sight available neutralise much of the situation awareness advantages US forces possess in other theatres. And the remaining orthodox response to such conditions, deploying 'overwhelming force' against an opponent, is precluded by the presence of large civilian populations and the ever-present risk of collateral damage. CTS seeks to address these problems by developing programs capable of automatically identifying vehicles by size, shape, colour and number plate, and by tracking and recording all vehicle movements in the combat zone. The driver's or passenger's facial features will also be recorded and (provided there is a photograph of the individual in the surveillance organisation's files) identified. Even without a formal identification, the presence of an individual or group of individuals in the same car, travelling the same route, at the same time each day, can be a valuable source of information. But Combat Zones That See is designed to do much more; it will number-crunch the totality of information obtained from all areas and all surveillance sources in the combat zone. Handling such an enormous data stream will allow CTS to perform higher-level inference and motion pattern analysis, identifying the enemy's activity structure (observation posts, supply points, sniper positions, etc) and predicting future activity.[8]

It is easy to see how valuable such an intelligence-gathering tool would be to hard-pressed US forces fighting in the warren of alleys that make up Baghdad's Sadr City. But we should be aware that many military innovations have found their way, and with a speed that sometimes astonishes, into civilian life. Combat Zones That See is designed specifically for urban use, and could easily be adapted for peace-time to provide blanket surveillance of movement in large cities. Used in this civilian context, the opportunities for abuse are obvious.

We've already seen in chapter 5 how CCTV cameras (which are relatively easy to spot) can be superseded in some surveillance situations by far more specific tracking of individuals which can now be routinely effected using passive RFID chips, read by ground-based scanners and even implanted in the body. In a further 'advance', the need for scanners has been removed, and the chip itself has been made 'active' with an almost limitless power source.

'Sky-Eye' is a microchip originally developed by Israeli researchers for intelligence use. Reportedly made of 'synthetic and organic fibre', it requires such a small amount of energy that it can use the body itself as a power source, and so function indefinitely. Once implanted under the skin, it is said to be invisible to the naked eye and to X-rays. A satellite or other remote monitoring device can track the individual carrying the chip, and locate him or her with a margin of error of 150 metres anywhere in the world. The technology has apparently been taken up with enthusiasm by many of the world's great and good, especially those who fear kidnapping and hope that the device will allow police to track them down quickly if they are abducted. The possibility that the kidnappers would have scanners to locate the chip and cut it from their captive's body (without anaesthetic?) has apparently never been considered.

It may be that the newly-apparent carcinogenic properties of implants (see p. 70) will swiftly remove this intrusive in-body technology, but at the moment they pose serious privacy and autonomy issues. While all such chips would presumably (though not necessarily) require an individual's consent to implant, we should expect a 'stealth strategy' of gradual implementation. The technology is already being used on the super-rich, and the 'poor man's Sky-Eye' – the passive RFID chip – is becoming more and more common. The latter device suffers from a systemic weakness, at least in the minds of technophiles, as the information it contains can only be accessed in the presence of a suitable reader. Sky-Eye solves this 'problem'; its satellite connection means that it can be tracked and accessed in the most remote locations. How long then, as Sky-Eye costs tumble, before 'at risk' humans, for example those suffering from such mental problems as Alzheimer's, are compulsorily 'chipped' with the new device for their own safety? Then, of course, many child abductions and lost-child scenarios would be obviated if all those under, say, twelve years of age were put online. Would a parent not be irresponsible for ignoring this potentially life-saving technology, which can locate the chipped individual anywhere in the world? With that accepted, how long might it be before the benefits of chipping all adults (in case of accidents while alone in the home, or for rescue if lost at sea or fell-walking) were seen to outweigh the 'notional' loss of privacy and freedom? And, in the way of things, chipped children would eventually grow up to be chipped adults. We may be at the start of a very slippery slope.

Of course, in the absence of CCTV surveillance or an implanted chip, the planned, ubiquitous ID card would locate you wherever there was a hidden RFID scanner. Not that the authorities really need an ID card to keep track of your movements; as we've seen in the present chapter, e-money, mobile phones, credit card surveillance and 'transaction trails' all form excellent, reliable back-ups to pinpoint your location and behaviour throughout the day. Harry Potter and his magical map are looking increasingly passé.

8

COMMUNICATION

Human beings are social creatures, and the sine qua non of such group behaviour is undoubtedly communication. We use gestures, facial expressions and posture to convey to others our mood and opinions, but by far the most precise and common method of communication between individuals of our species is language. Written or spoken, language is absolutely indispensable to the huge, complex urban societies in which most of the world's population now lives. In a host of different ways, language defines what we are and what we have become.

The detailed organisation and planning necessary for the efficient functioning of such super-cities, and for much else in modern life, including trade, politics, defence and socialisation (or entertainment), is inconceivable without the ability to transcend the natural limitations of our linguistic abilities: we need to be able to communicate outside normal voice-range. From the very first runner, carrying an oral or written message from one person to another, much human effort has been devoted to the pursuit of speedy distant communication. The hackneyed phrase remains true: information *is* power. To be first with the news meant success in war, love and business. Equally, being able to intercept such messages and know their content before the intended recipient conferred an even greater advantage. The holy grail of those seeking dominion over others has always been total access to the communications of friend and foe alike.

Ironically, it is our modern ability to communicate electronically over vast distances and in huge numbers that has allowed the development of systems that can listen in to any written or verbal electronic correspondence, and record, transcribe and store the conversation. And all without the originators of the conversation even knowing that an eavesdropper has been present.

Government calling

Wire taps and mail intercepts are the stuff of spy movies and drug-busts. Most terrorist and narcotics operations require a high degree of coordination, which in turn necessitates detailed communication – listening in on the bad guys is an invaluable tool in law enforcement. But while in the past wire taps and the opening of mail were legally subject to judicial approval and oversight, and required 'boots on the ground' to physically connect the apparatus (thereby limiting the number of taps that could be performed), today any number of organisations have the right to examine telephonic communications, and computer technology allows huge numbers of phone calls, faxes and emails to be processed simultaneously.

Mike Devine discovered the reality of the surveillance web on 2 June 2004, when Special Branch officers raided his office, slapped on the handcuffs and took him away for questioning. His crime? An incriminating text message he had sent earlier which said:

> How about this for Tommy Gun? OK – so let's agree about the price and make it one jet airliner and ten prisoners.

The Special Branch considered Devine a potential terrorist until he explained that he and his friends play in a Clash tribute band. One of the group could not remember the words of the Clash song 'Tommy Gun', and Devine had sent a text message with the missing (and admittedly suspicious-sounding) words. But how did the security forces know the content of Devine's innocent (and private) message? Special Branch claimed that the message unaccountably went astray, and was sent to a Bristol woman who then alerted the authorities. But terrorism expert Chris Dobson believes the incident demonstrates that GCHQ is monitoring every vocal and textual mobile phone message.[1]

Email surveillance in the UK is now a reality. The Regulation of Investigatory Powers Act (RIPA) has been steadily added to, allowing an increasing number of government departments to access private citizens' communication records. There was uproar recently over proposals to let anyone in the UK police, of sergeant rank or above, authorise the viewing of private email. Despite this, hundreds of organisations, including government departments, NHS trusts and local councils, already have powers to carry out covert surveillance. To understand the enormity of this intrusive legislation, we should imagine our reaction if all our 'paper mail' – letters, parcels and telegrams – could be opened and viewed by any town hall official. And in most circumstances, we would not even be aware that such surveillance had taken place.

Universities regularly hold copies of all emails sent by students. And should the student be studying for a PhD in Information Technology and be able to encrypt his missive so that only his chosen recipient may decipher the message, the law will soon step in. Under the RIPA, it's a criminal offence to withhold from government agencies the use of a key that would allow them to decrypt data for which they have a valid warrant. All emails are therefore potentially readable by the government. The penalty for ignoring the legislation is two years in prison.

Even more revealing was the shocking inadvertent disclosure that proceeded from the 1997 trial of two peace campaigners who were appealing against a conviction for trespassing at the notorious United States 'Communications Relay Centre' at Menwith Hill, the town that, officially, does not exist. Despite a population of at least 1,400 permanent staff and their families, including engineers, physicists, mathematicians, linguists and computer scientists (plus over 370 Ministry of Defence staff), all of whom live on a base which boasts houses, shops, schools, a chapel and a sports centre, the site is merely hinted at on civilian road maps. The 560-acre site is a little bit of the United States tucked away in the hills near Harrogate in North Yorkshire. Only US passport holders are allowed access to many parts of the site, which is under the authority of that nation's National Security Agency (NSA). Surrounded by watchtowers, CCTV cameras and razor wire, and dotted with 23 radomes (the 'giant golfballs' which protect sensitive listening devices), Menwith Hill is the largest, best-funded and most sophisticated listening post on the planet.

Menwith Hill is a child of the Cold War, designed to listen in to Russian and Warsaw Pact communications, but with the demise of the Soviet bloc the secretive base turned its sensitive ears to other targets. Its giant radomes, masts and satellite dishes scan the horizon, 24 hours a day, 365 days of the year, picking up on all kinds of electronic communications, listening in to drug dealers, terrorists and, as the appeal of the two peace activists discovered, to the telephone conversations of everyone in the UK. During the appeal, in 'documents and testimony submitted by British Telecom ... Mr R.G. Morris, BT's head of Emergency Planning, revealed that at least three major domestic fibre-optic telephone trunk lines – each capable of carrying

100,000 calls simultaneously – were wired through Menwith Hill, allowing the NSA to tap into the very heart of the British Telecom network.'[2] This embarrassing piece of information was swiftly stamped upon. Judge Jonathan Crabtree, who was overseeing the appeal, censured BT and prohibited Mr Morris from giving further evidence, citing reasons of national security.

This revelation caused a furore in the press at the time, and not without good reason. For let us be clear about this: British Telecom, presumably at the behest of whichever British government was in power at the time, has aided and abetted a foreign power to wiretap the British nation. Thanks to their work, the NSA at any given time can simultaneously eavesdrop on the conversations of at least 300,000 UK citizens. And succeeding governments have colluded in the practice. This is surely a step too far in the 'special relationship'.

But the truth is that the 'BT connection' is just a small part of Menwith Hill's surveillance activity, and that Menwith Hill itself is merely a small segment in the greatest communications surveillance project of all time – Echelon.

The Echelon system

The Echelon project is undoubtedly the most comprehensive listening device on the face of the globe – a satellite-based global electronic surveillance system, capable of capturing and analysing virtually every phone call, email, fax and telex in Europe and North America and beyond. Echelon is controlled by the United States' NSA and operated in conjunction with Britain's GCHQ, with help from the Canadian, Australian and New Zealand security services.

The roots of the Echelon system lie buried in the message interception and code-breaking battles of World War II. The work of the UK government's Code and Cipher School at Bletchley Park, especially the use of Alan Turing's electro-mechanical bombe in cracking Germany's 'unbreakable' Enigma cipher, emphasised the importance of computational science in SIGINT (Signal Intelligence) programmes. With the defeat of Germany and arrival of the Cold War, SIGINT agencies were given a new foe on which to turn their burgeoning skills in message interception. It was soon realised that to ensure the most efficient use of resources, the Western allies needed to act in unison. Between 1946 and 1947, the intelligence agencies of the British Empire were brought together under the auspices of the Commonwealth SIGINT Organisation, which comprised Britain, Canada, Australia and New Zealand. In 1947, the still-secret UKUSA (pronounced You-koo-sa) agreement between Britain and the United States (with the USA the senior party) defined the intelligence relationships and responsibilities of the partners.

In essence, the Western allies divided up the world into their respective 'listening zones'. The British GCHQ covers Europe (including Russia west of the Ural Mountains) and Africa. Australia's Defence Signals Directorate (DSD) watches over South East Asia, the eastern Indian Ocean and the south-west Pacific zones. New Zealand's Government Communications Security Bureau scans the airwaves in the southern Pacific, while NSA facilities in the US cover traffic from both North and South America. The Canadian listening posts, run by the Communications Security Establishment (CSE), act as a back-stop for the NSA and GCHQ, intercepting communications from northern Europe (including northern Russia), and North American signals.

Position intercept stations belonging to these nations form a vast electronic net that captures all satellite, radio frequency, microwave, cellular and fibre-optic communications. Land-based

124

radio listening posts are scattered across the globe, located at military posts, often on foreign soil; intelligence ships criss-cross the ocean, sucking in all manner of broadcasts and sifting them for evidence of military communications and position data of 'enemy' assets. There are even submarines which scour the ocean deep and 'wiretap' undersea communications cables.[3]

But by far the most important of all these surveillance tools are listening and reception stations pointed at the world's communication satellites, such as the score of Intelsat satellites that lie in geostationary orbit above particular areas on the earth's equator. Echelon bases tap into the traffic carried by these satellites, looking for information of interest to the intelligence services. A further plank in the surveillance platform are US spy satellites such as the Mercury, Mentor and Trumpet satellite series, circling up to 20,000 miles above our heads and hoovering up microwave, radio, cellphone and radio transmissions. 'The downlink stations that control the operations and targeting of these satellites are under the exclusive control of the United States, despite their location on foreign military bases.'[4] The main downlink stations are two in number: Pine Gap in Australia, and our old friend Menwith Hill in Yorkshire, UK.

Impressive though the interception of almost all the world's communications undoubtedly is, it is what happens once the data is downloaded that makes Echelon such an effective spy tool.

The sheer mass of information streaming into Menwith Hill and Pine Gap defies the imagination. But the systems in place at these two sites are able to sift, decrypt and categorise the incoming stream of millions of messages, flagging up potentially important signals for further analysis by UKUSA agents. The bulk of raw data is fed into enormous supercomputers (including Lockheed Corporation's SILKWORTH at Menwith Hill), where it is processed through advanced software, such as voice recognition programs which convert speech into text. One system, VOICECAST, recognises an individual's speech profile and automatically records any call made by them. From there, programs such as MAGISTRAND and PATHFINDER use complex algorithms to sort through the text documents in search of key words or phrases. Because different geographical locations may have different surveillance priorities, each station maintains its own 'Dictionary' or list of keywords, which is altered on a regular basis. Once any current keyword is found by the system, the computer records and transcribes the communication and flags it for future analysis by human operatives. Enormous numbers of analysts and codebreakers (the NSA is the largest employer of mathematicians in the world) use the information to compile the reports, 'gists' and summaries, a concise distillation of facts and opinions that are Echelon's true raison d'être. UKUSA participants who might find a particular message, or analysis, of interest are sent copies via PLATFORM, a global computer system that supports the entire Echelon system.

This was all well and good when the Russian Bear was in the ascendancy, and the West faced nuclear Armageddon or the prospect of a Soviet armoured thrust into the heart of Western Europe. The Russians had their own communications intercept strategy and if the USA and its allies excelled its adversary in this field, few people on this side of the Iron Curtain were complaining. But with the fall of the Soviet Empire, this massive spy network faced cutbacks and budget reductions. Echelon needed new legitimate targets to spy upon and these were duly found in the form of drug barons and terrorists. Leaving aside the question of whether this multi-billion-dollar enterprise has made as many inroads against the drug-smuggling industry as it might, narcotics has been effectively sidelined by the US administration's 'war on terror' following the 9/11 attack on the World Trade Centre (of which more later). Echelon's ability to identify transmissions from terrorist organisations and listen in on their plans has seriously dented the offensive capabilities of Islamic jihadists and similar groups. Al Qaeda reportedly eschews all electronic communications for its high-level planning, preferring to send human operatives to deliver oral instructions to its groups.

Few would quibble with the use of Echelon for such purposes. Unfortunately, it seems the temptations involved in being able to listen in to all the world's conversations have in some cases proved impossible to resist.

It has been alleged that the NSA uses the Echelon system to spy on political figures within the USA, to further US commercial interests worldwide, and even, despite specific Constitutional prohibition, to listen in on the communications of all US citizens. Even as early as 1975, the late senator for Idaho, Frank Church, who was at that time chairman of the select committee on intelligence, investigated the agency and came away appalled by the power of the NSA.

'That capability at any time could be turned around on the American people,' he stated after his investigation, 'and no American would have any privacy left, such is the capability to monitor everything: telephone conversations, telegrams, it doesn't matter. There would be no place to hide.' If a dictatorship ever took over the United States, the NSA 'could enable it to impose total tyranny, and there would be no way to fight back. I don't want to see this country ever go across the bridge,' Senator Church said. 'I know the capacity that is there to make tyranny total in America, and we must see to it that this agency and all agencies that possess this technology operate within the law and under proper supervision, so that we never cross over that abyss. That is the abyss from which there is no return.'[5]

We should remember that this was said over 30 years ago, before the age of mobile phones, personal computers and email (and much else besides) made even more of our correspondence and conversations accessible to electronic eavesdropping. Yet despite the senator's stern warning, monitoring of US citizens continues.

In 1995 Michael Barnes, a former Maryland congressman, claimed that his phone conversations had been taped on a regular basis during the presidency of Ronald Reagan. This was a repeat of a claim, made in a 1988 Cleveland *Plain Dealer* article by a US operative at Menwith Hill, that she had listened in on the real-time phone conversations of South Carolina senator Strom Thurmond. Between these two US exposés, in 1992 GCHQ officers approached the *Observer* newspaper to report their concern that Greenpeace, Amnesty International and several Christian organisations had all been added to the Echelon Dictionary as groups worthy of surveillance.

Thus far – or at least since 1975, when Senate Intelligence Committee hearings revealed the existence of illegal surveillance records on numerous US citizens, and Congressional oversight was instituted with reasonable effect – only political figures and political or quasi-political organisations have been targeted by those controlling the Echelon machine. Ordinary US citizens have been, as far as we know, scrupulously left out of the surveillance loop.

Freedom slipped another notch in 2005, when the *New York Times* revealed that the NSA had been spying on American citizens. Citing various anonymous sources, the newspaper claimed that President Bush had signed a secret order authorising the interception (without judicial oversight) of phone calls and emails from US nationals in communication with persons outside the country. After the story broke, White House spokesmen cited a September 2001 Congressional resolution authorising the so-called 'war on terror' as its justification for conducting warrantless domestic surveillance – despite the fact that federal law specifically forbids such activity.

It seems that the prediction of the late Senator Frank Church – that Echelon's capabilities were a direct threat to the freedoms of the American people – is well on its way to being proved correct. All this is, of course, a strictly internal matter for the USA. And while the good citizens of the Land of the Free have waxed righteously indignant about illegal communications surveillance on themselves, they seem quite at ease with the concept of their security arms doing precisely the same thing to the rest of the world, friend and foe alike. And on the use of Echelon for commercial espionage in favour of the USA there has been a deafening silence.

According to Patrick Poole, spying on foreign companies has been brought within Echelon's ambit by the simple expedient of redefining the concept of 'national security' to include economic, commercial and corporate interests.[6] The US Department of Commerce has even created an Office of Intelligence Liaison whose primary function is to pass on intercepts of commercial interest to US corporations, courtesy of the NSA and others. The beneficiaries, in many cases, are said to be those businesses that worked with the NSA to provide components of the Echelon system. 'This incestuous relationship is so strong, that sometimes this intelligence information is used to push other American manufacturers out of deals in favour of these mammoth US defence and intelligence contractors who frequently are the source of major cash contributions to both political parties.' Former head of the CIA James Woolsey has admitted that the US does secretly collect information on European companies. But he insisted that only businesses that violated United Nations sanctions or offered bribes to gain contracts were targeted (from the *Guardian*, 8 April 2000).

The USA does not like others discussing Echelon. As early as 1998, the European Green Party claimed that an EU discussion on the Echelon system and its misuse in Europe had been deferred owing to American pressure. Britain takes a similar line, and in spring 2000 tried to stifle EU debate on Echelon by warning the other EU states that their own dirty linen would be aired in any discussion. The Portuguese had called for the debate, a demand supported by French eurocrats incensed by reports that the US had beaten the European consortium Airbus to a deal with Saudi Arabia by using Echelon's eavesdropping capabilities. Despite the UK's threats, the EU set up an ad hoc committee of enquiry, leading to a report by the European Parliament on Echelon. The report's findings made sobering reading, and in 2004 resulted in the EU's decision to invest €11 million over the following four years to develop secure communications based on quantum cryptography (which will use physical laws governing the universe on the smallest scale to create unbreakable encryption keys). Sergio Cova, a professor from the electronics department of Milan Polytechnic and one of the project's coordinators, explained: 'The aim is to produce a communication system that cannot be intercepted by anyone, and that includes Echelon.' No one is yet sure that the project is feasible – significant technical innovations and scientific advances will be required to make it work – but the size of the EU investment serves to underline the seriousness with which it takes the threat posed by the Echelon system. Christian Monyk, the overall coordinator of the project, was frank about its aims. 'This is an effort to cope with Echelon,' he said, citing the damage caused to European companies in the past by economic espionage. 'With this project we will be making an essential contribution to the economic independence of Europe.'[7]

The spy in your computer

We have already seen how systems such as Echelon can monitor electronic communications, including the email we send and receive each day from our computers, Blackberries and mobiles. All these platforms for email communication are internet-dependent, and the ease with which our electronic correspondence can be monitored gives an indication of just how porous the world wide web really is. Intriguingly, the internet traces its origins back to a 1969 US Defense Department project, which aimed to prevent loss of communications after an enemy (notably nuclear) attack. The Defense Advanced Research Projects Agency (DARPA) subsequently launched the DARPA Internet Program, the management of which was eventually transferred to the Defense Communications Agency. The internet is, in effect, a child of the US military.

Internet monitoring

The internet's open structure means that government and business can easily view and record all our internet activity. All websites log information about who visits them and when, recording your unique 'IP address' and time of every visit. 'Subway Serenade', a street musician in New York, posted this startling information at 1.16 pm on 28 May 2006:

> On my website I have a traffic meter that in most cases gives me the longitude and latitude of each visitor's IP address. I then paste this information into Google Earth and in a few seconds I'm hovering 300 meters above their house and have the name of the street where it's located. For me it's just amusement to see where from around the world my visitors come, and I'm

thoroughly harmless. But if a simple busker can do this so effort-
lessly, I wonder about those not so easily entertained ...

Location aside, the monitoring of our internet wanderings is
child's play. While it remains difficult to physically tap into a
telephone connection, the nodal nature of the internet means
that such invasive activity is unnecessary; all that is required
is monitoring of the hub to which your line connects, in practice your internet service provider (ISP). Eavesdrop on all ISPs
in any particular country, and you have access to everything
that every citizen of that state does on the net. Extend that
process to other countries, and the browsing and e-commerce
of whole continents can be quickly and easily surveilled. Indeed,
this has already been accomplished for Europe. On 15 March
2006 the European Union passed Directive 2006/24/EC, which
made it mandatory for ISPs to hold the data traffic of all their
customers for a period of two years. Every website visited,
every e-commerce transaction, every email sent – all recorded
and stored for every one of the EU's 450 million citizens with
access to the Internet.

Another feature of the system, the Internet Gateway, provides
additional opportunities for the monitoring and censorship of
our surfing activities. This has been likened to a door by which
internet access to and from any given country can be controlled.
According to one human rights organisation, China has installed
a system known as the Great Firewall, by which the Ministry
of Public Security controls internet access for the entire 1.3
billion strong population of China. Recently the Chinese government said it intended to replace the Great Firewall system with
Golden Shield. China will now build surveillance intelligence
into the network, allowing it to 'see', 'hear' and 'think'. Content-
filtration will shift from the national level to millions of digital
information and communications devices in public places and

people's homes.[8] The technology behind Golden Shield is incredibly complex and is based on research undertaken largely by Western technology firms, including Nortel Networks, Sun Microsystems, Cisco and others.[9]

These developments, Echelon in the 'free' West and Golden Shield in 'communist' China, each undertaken with the help of Western businesses, are in breach of national legislation and at least two articles of the Universal Declaration of Human Rights:

Article 12: No one shall be subject to arbitrary interference with his privacy, family, home or correspondence, nor to attacks upon his honour and reputation. Everyone has the right to the protection of the law against such interference or attacks.

Article 19: Everyone has the right to freedom of opinion and expression; this right includes the freedom to hold opinions without interference and to seek, receive and impart information and ideas through any media and regardless of frontiers.

Nor are private companies far behind governments in taking an interest in your personal correspondence. The internet search engine Google launched Gmail in 2004, with the carrot of 1GB of free storage space. However, the privacy agreement 'enables Google to access the contents of your email messages with the intention of providing relevant advertising on the sidebars'. That is, they read your mail, decide what you are interested in, and sell advertising space to companies hoping you will purchase their products. It was not possible to join Gmail without agreeing to this 'privacy statement'.

But will Google use this data for other purposes? Well, maybe; the short answer is you have to trust them. Gmail's terms of use stated:

> Google may, in its sole discretion, modify or revise these terms and conditions and policies at any time, and you agree to be bound by such modifications or revisions. If you do not accept and abide by this Agreement, you may not use the Gmail service.

So ... having effectively signed a blank cheque, if the company decides to change its 'terms and conditions and policies' you are, quite simply, stuck with it. Your emails and the accompanying analysis could be sold off to the nearest profiling company (see next chapter) and you none the wiser.

Would they do it? It's hard to say. The company has been widely condemned for bowing to pressure from China to remove websites considered 'political' by the Chinese government. Rival company Yahoo! is the subject of a 2007 US court challenge by the mother of Shi Tao, a Chinese journalist and democracy campaigner, jailed for ten years in 2005 for leaking state secrets to foreigners after Yahoo! handed over server logs to Beijing. Yahoo! claims it would have faced prosecution itself had it not cooperated with the Chinese government. The action caused outrage, and led to a resolution from New York pension funds calling on the Yahoo! board to adopt stronger policies on freedom of speech and against data-mining by governments.[10]

Internet search engines are also at the forefront of another privacy-busting strategy that can be found on almost any computer – the not-so-tasty 'cookie'.

The term 'cookie' derives from a Unix program, 'Fortune Cookie', that produces a different message, or fortune, each time it runs. These 'bite-sized' pieces of software are sent down the telephone line when you connect to a website (e.g. AOL) and sit quietly and surreptitiously in your computer. Essentially, a cookie is a mechanism that allows a website to record your comings and goings, usually without your knowledge or consent, and this data can be sold to target advertisements more specifically to your tastes. Put even more plainly, 'the [web] pages you read tell marketers what junk to push on you'.[11] When you surf the net, the cookie connects with the parent website and sends back details of every webpage and newsgroup visited, every e-commerce purchase made, every email you send, as well as any information you've volunteered, such as your name, address and interests. If you are aware of the cookie and have the expertise to switch it off, another is sent down the line (without your consent) the very next time you connect to the site, and begins its 'profiling' job once again. There are of course legitimate uses for cookies, such as mass customisation of the content on websites. But it's not generally possible to tell, from looking at a cookie alone, how it will be used. If you have ever wondered how a website can use your name to greet you, it's because you have a cookie in your computer sending that, and probably lots more, information to your server. It is instructive to check your browser for these silent spies in your computer – the number often runs into the hundreds.

There would be far less concern about cookies, and much else besides, if the data they obtained was held solely by the commercial organisation that collected it. But in the brave new world of electronic commerce, data from an enormous number of sources is being sold, aggregated and analysed by a new industry, euphemistically entitled Customer Relations Management, whose remit is the profiling of the populations of entire countries.

9

LIFESTYLE

In 1996 a Texas grandmother, Beverly Dennis, received a letter from a man she had never met. The letter discussed her divorce, her salary, her hobbies, the magazines she read and other personal details. The anonymous writer assailed her with an elaborate and degrading sexual fantasy involving the brand of hand lotion she used, and closed the letter with a chilling 'when I get out I might come see you'.

Who was this man? How had he targeted Beverly Dennis? And how was he privy to her home address and so many of her personal details? Ms Dennis decided to find out, and what she discovered led to a celebrated case and class action against the direct marketing firm Metromail.[1] It turned out that the company had been making the best use of its resources by employing prisoners to upload her personal details, and those of thousands of others, into Metromail's massive profiling system. The writer of the letter was a convicted burglar and rapist.

Perhaps most chilling of all was Metromail's take on the incident. Despite having accumulated 25 pages of personal data on Beverly Dennis, 'including when she had used medication for haemorrhoids', during litigation Metromail claimed that they had not violated the woman's privacy, that they had no duty to inform individuals that prisoners were processing their personal data, and that the data processed was not highly intimate or embarrassing.[2] As a result of the court case, Metromail ceased using prisoners to upload personal information. But the collection of data continues.

Metromail sold information on 90 per cent of US households and, according to its own promotional material, collected data on 67,000 babies weekly from 3,200 sources. That this information was available to anyone willing to pay was revealed in the 'Klaas Scandal' when a KCBS-TV reporter bought the personal information of 5,000 children from the company with a $277 money order, using the name Richard Allan Davis, an individual who was at that time on trial in San Jose, California for the kidnap and murder of twelve-year-old Polly Klaas in 1993 (he was later convicted). No proof of identity was required by Metromail, and the 'child killer' obtained details on 5,000 children by return of post.

Metromail is not the only firm accumulating data on children. Lifestyle Change Communications of Atlanta has data on 33 million-plus children. Best Mailing Lists of Tucson sells the names, ages and telephone numbers of 22 million children. There are many others. Child-oriented data is simply one small facet of the hidden world of 'profiling'.

Private profiles

Profiling is a little documented surveillance technique, used as a means of generating prospective customers, or suspects, from within a large diverse population. In essence, a set of characteristics relating to a particular group of individuals is generated, using information derived from past experience with other individuals from the same target group. Once this is established, a database is then searched for persons who conform closely to this set of characteristics. The technology has the previously impossible ability to select target groups for specific interests and activities from a huge population base.

In the private sector, the technique is extensively used to identify potential customers, those most likely to buy a specific product or service. The companies that do this work divide the population into a hierarchical pyramid of finer and finer distinctions, which allow for the precise targeting of products and services. In the USA, the Claritas company recognises fifteen major groups, such as the affluent 'Elite Suburbs' through 'Affluentials' and 'Urban Midscale', all the way down to 'Second City Blues' and 'Rustic Living'. Each category is further subdivided into sub-classes; 'Elite Suburbs', for example, breaks down into 'Blue Blood Estates', 'Winner's Circle', 'Executive Suites', 'Pools & Patios' and 'Kids & Cul-de-sacs'. The categories may change from time to time, but the aim remains the same: to identify specific groups who share a constellation of attributes that can be exploited by marketing departments. Obviously, a company stands a better chance of selling a top-of-the-range Cadillac to an 'Elite Suburb' than to a member of 'Small Downtown' or 'Family Scramble' (two of the four sub-categories from 'Second City Blues').

But profiling companies do more than categorise your socio-economic group and lifestyle. They generate 'compiled lists' – databases formed from a whole host of different records (*internal data* garnered from cookies, credit transactions, focus groups, customer surveys, promotional contests, loyalty cards and the like, and *external data* generated from membership lists, telephone directories, public records and other national statistics), combining this information with their existing databases to further refine the sensitivity of their targeting – and form, simultaneously, a comprehensive and at times intrusive 'file' on any particular person. The range of attributes

139

linked to an individual's identity is enormous; in the USA the Electronic Privacy Information Centre (EPIC) gives the following list:

TABLE 1: ATTRIBUTES LINKED TO IDENTITY

- Social Security number
- Shopping preferences
- Health information, including diet type, allergies, arthritis, incontinence/bladder problems, diabetes, hearing loss, prostate problems, visual impairment and birth defects
- Marital status
- Financial situation (solvency, creditworthiness, loan amounts, credit cards)
- Date of birth
- Sex
- Age
- Household income
- Race and ethnicity
- Geography
- Physical characteristics such as height and weight
- Household occupants (whether an individual has children)
- Telephone number
- Utility usage (electric or gas usage, telephone usage, cable or satellite usage, internet subscription, cellular phone usage)
- Magazine subscriptions
- Occupation
- Level of education
- Whether an individual is likely to respond to 'money-making opportunities'
- Congressional district

- Size of clothes worn
- Habits (smoking)
- Arrest records
- Lifestyle preferences
- Hobbies (whether and what the individual collects)
- Religion (affiliation and denomination)
- Homeownership
- Characteristics of residence (size, number of bedrooms and bathrooms, sale price, rent and mortgage payments)
- Type of automobile owned
- Characteristics of automobile owned (year, make, value, fuel type, number of cylinders, presence of vanity or special membership plates)
- Whether the individual responds to direct mail solicitations
- Contributions to political, religious and charitable groups
- Membership in book, video tape and compact disc clubs
- Mail order purchases and type
- Product ownership (beeper, contact lenses, electronics, fitness equipment, recreational equipment)
- Pet ownership and type
- Interests (including gambling, arts, antiques, astrology)
- Book preferences
- Music preferences
- 'Socialites'

(Source: 'Privacy & Consumer Profiling', EPIC, 13 October 2004)

It seems there is nothing in anyone's private life that cannot be prised from the records, ordered, collated and turned into a dossier to be sold to the highest bidder. In medical marketing, EPIC gives a list of around 70 ailments that are routinely researched and linked to individuals by profilers seeking to sell to pharmaceutical and other companies (see table 2 overleaf).

TABLE 2: AILMENTS TARGETED

- Allergy – nasal
- Allergies – wheat
- Alzheimer's (incl. adult care-giver)
- Arthritis
- Asthma
- Athlete's foot
- Breast cancer
- Bronchitis
- Cancer
- Celiac sprue
- Chewing and swallowing difficulties
- Chronic back pain
- Clinical depression
- Colon cancer
- Constipation
- Contact lenses
- Crohn's disease
- Dandruff
- Dentures
- Diabetes – all (types 1 and 2)
- Dry/flaky skin
- Eczema
- Emphysema
- Epilepsy
- Frequent chapped lips
- Frequent cold sores
- Frequent flu
- Fungal infections
- Fungus infections – nail/foot
- GERD/acid reflux/ulcers
- Gingivitis
- Glasses
- Glaucoma
- Hair loss/baldness
- Headaches
- Hearing impaired/hearing aid
- Heart attack
- Heartburn/acid indigestion
- Heart disease
- High blood pressure
- High cholesterol
- Hyperthyroidism
- Impotence/ED
- Incontinence – urine
- Insomnia
- Irritable bowel syndrome
- Lactose intolerance
- Low protein disorder
- Lyme disease
- Menopause
- Menstrual cramps
- Migraines
- Motion sickness
- Multiple sclerosis
- Obesity
- Osteoporosis
- Parkinson's disease
- Prostate cancer
- Psoriasis
- Rheumatoid arthritis
- Rosacea
- Sensitive teeth
- Shingles
- Spinal cord injury
- Ulcerative colitis
- Ulcers
- Wheelchair use
- Yeast infection

(Source: 'Privacy & Consumer Profiling', EPIC, 13 October 2004)

Medical Marketing Services will sell lists of those suffering with all these diseases, 'cross-referenced with information regarding age, educational level, family dwelling size, gender, income, lifestyle, marital status and presence of children'. One company, Experian, which at one time owned Metromail (they merged in 1998), has among its 'products' a list of incontinence sufferers. Yet another marketing business, Dr Leonard's Lifeline, states that:

> The Dr Leonard's Healthcare File has been overlayed [*sic*] with data to identify the ethnic and religious backgrounds of their customers. These mature buyers are responsive mail order buyers who purchase high quality, attractively priced products to enhance their lives. Product line includes health care, pain relief, personal care and home accessories.

Another informative marketing company is Dunhill International Lists, who offer everything from the heights of 'Affluent America' ('the most comprehensive database of millionaires, multi-millionaires and billionaires and their wealthiest neighbours ...') to the downtown misery of 'Sub-Prime Auto Loan Applicants' ('Many have had their loan applications [auto, home, credit card] rejected due to poor credit history ... These individuals are in dire need of credit').

Lists of Catholics who make charitable donations, lists of Catholics who subscribe to *Newsweek*, lists of consumer magazine subscribers, lists of accredited investors in the UK, lists of affluent women approaching retirement; there is a list or database for every marketing desire, and no end to the marketing agencies' desire for more and more information about us. And it comes as some surprise to discover just where much of this information is derived.

143

Product warranty cards

In these modern times, virtually any product worth more than £20 (and a lot costing less than that) comes with a 'product warranty card' which you are required to complete in order to be able to claim on the warranty should anything go wrong with your purchase. That, at least, is what the manufacturers want us to think. The truth is that you do not even have to send the warranty card off to them. It is sufficient to hold the card, plus your receipt, for your rights to be safeguarded.

Why, then, the implied threat of voiding the guarantee if you fail to post the card? Look closely at the details requested on the document; in most cases they will seem a little over the top. Why should a company selling, say, an electric kettle need to know your date of birth, your postcode and various other irrelevant details about you and your lifestyle? Some cards are extremely intrusive, with queries on number of children in a family, personal income and even questions on hobbies and health problems. Why?

The answer is that the details you send back on the warranty card are valuable profiling information, and are sold on by the company to marketing agencies. They may only get 'a nickel a name', but the volume of sales means such data transactions add up to a considerable sum for even medium-sized businesses.

Store loyalty cards

Every large retailer, from supermarkets to DIY stores, now seems to be offering loyalty cards, granting either 'points' or discounts with every purchase within the store. While the companies trumpet their card-linked offers in advertisements, what is not mentioned is the fact that the ubiquitous 'store card' is an absolute goldmine of useful information on each buyer. The cards record every purchase over long periods of time and can be used to profile customers' purchasing preferences and (more worryingly) to form a profile of his/her personality or lifestyle. And as many of the larger supermarkets have branched out into selling pharmaceuticals, alcohol, books, CDs, DVDs and clothes, as well as the more usual foodstuffs, the amount of information collected on each individual can be vast.

This not a simple matter of the store using the data to determine what is selling best, whether you prefer Heinz beans to any other variety. Such analysis will of course be performed on the data and is perfectly harmless. What is of concern is the selling on of loyalty card information from millions of customers to data-aggregating companies, who will overlay the data with other databases to create detailed profiles on each named shopper. There are now publishing firms producing mail-order catalogues in which the pages are printed to suit the preferences of each client in the database. You may get a catalogue full of sports equipment, while your technology-mad neighbour will receive an 'identical' publication brimming with computers and scanners. You may not feel uneasy that the database company knows so much about you – you may even perceive it a positive advantage to have your interests and needs anticipated – nor is it a worry if Tesco knows you like Heinz beans. But you may well consider it an inexcusable invasion of privacy if a marketing firm uses this same database to discover if you are a regular buyer of face or haemorrhoid cream, or whether you purchase nappies for your child or for yourself (as we've seen, Metromail detailed haemorrhoid cream purchases, and Experian is happy to sell any company willing to pay the asking price a database of individuals who are incontinent).

Cards are also divisive. If you are a top shopper, i.e. spend more money, your discount offers will be higher than those offered to the bottom 10 per cent of spenders. In the Philippines, they've taken this analysis to extremes. The top 5 per cent of shoppers in Rustin Supercenter's 'ShopWise' stores earn an 'elite' card which gives them special perks such as exclusive carts. Donnie Tantoco, an executive at Rustin, explained some of the other benefits: 'They also have check-out areas exclusive for their use so they don't have to fall in line too long. We also give them gifts and they are offered free snacks and coffee while waiting, aside from getting additional discounts on selected items. We are also more liberal in our return policy toward them, albeit there are no cases of returns so far.' He added another telling comment: 'Over time, loyal customers become less price sensitive.'[3]

Other loyalty card aficionados have noted this also. A Fujitsu representative explained the merits of his company's 'smart card': 'The other way it's useful is that if I have your shopping habits and I know in a category, for instance, that you're a loyal customer of Coca-Cola, let's say, then basically, when I advertise Coca-Cola to you the discount's going to be different [i.e. lower] than if I know that you're ... somebody that's price sensitive.'[4]

The store card's effect on the face of retailing was well described by Professor Joseph Turow of the University of Pennsylvania's Annenberg School for Communication:

> The idea used to be that you, the consumer, could shop around, compare goods and prices, and make a smart choice. But now the reverse is also true: the vendor looks at its consumer base, gathers information, and decides whether you are worth pleasing, or whether it can profit from your loyalty and habits ... This all might make sense for retailers. But for the rest of us, it can feel like our simple corner store is turning into a Marrakech

bazaar – except that the merchant has been reading our diary, while we're negotiating blindfolded, behind a curtain, through a translator.

Retailers and their suppliers spend much time persuading the customer to buy into these card schemes. The latest must-have is a smart cart, of which Fujitsu's 'U-Scan Shopper' is the latest and most advanced. Using up to 100 infra-red guide posts, the 6.5-inch flat-screen device – bolted to a shopping cart and rendered brat-proof with a surrounding quarter-inch of hardened Mylar plastic – leads the customer around the store, flagging up promotions as they approach the relevant aisle, suggesting new recipes and, as they scan in their own purchases, updating the shopping list in real time. As an added bonus, the U-Scan will transmit 'side orders' to the deli or pharmacy sections and tell the customer when they are ready to be picked up.

Fujitsu have even addressed privacy concerns: the U-Scan Shopper system allows you to remain anonymous, or you can use a loyalty card. But without the card, 'the system's CRM [Customer Relationship Management] capabilities – a big draw for retailers – are virtually nil'.[5] Denied the ability to collect reams of valuable data from each customer, it is unlikely that a company shelling out around £650 for each cart will ever enable the anonymity mode. Vernon Slack, Fujitsu's director of mobile solutions, hinted at a stealth approach to marketing the smart cart, stating that in an initial deployment, requiring a loyalty card will turn off more privacy-suspicious, time-crunched customers than it will attract. However, once established as a normal part of supermarket 'furniture', it is more than probable that the smart-cart's anonymity option will simply disappear.

Are profiles accurate?

Given that data marketing 'dossiers' on an individual can affect that individual's life in a number of serious ways (e.g. in establishing their credit rating), it is important to know just how accurate this new 'science' of profiling really is. Surprisingly, there does not appear to have been any serious attempt to use a statistically significant cohort of individuals and to assess their dossiers against their true situation in life. However, it is known that self-reporting – such as the filling in of warranty cards – is inherently biased; people regularly claim far higher salaries than they earn, for example, and are apt to boast of interesting or exciting pastimes in which they do not participate. In April 2001 Richard Smith, a former Privacy Foundation chief technical officer, asked to see the dossier held on him by ChoicePoint, a 'leading provider of identification and credential verification services for business and government' according to their own PR blurb. Worryingly, after reading the file, Smith concluded that the dossier contained 'more misinformation than correct information'.

But accurate information is no guarantee of an accurate assessment. On 10 August 2004 the wife of Lieutenant Philip Lyons, a 25-year veteran of Tukwila Fire Department, saw flames coming from beneath the bay window of their home on Mountlake Terrace near Seattle, USA. Lieutenant Lyons called the emergency services immediately, but put out the fire himself using a garden hose. Seventeen days later, he was astounded when he found himself charged with first-degree attempted arson of his own home. According to the *Seattle Times*, a major plank in the case against Lyons was the data stored by his Safeway Club Card of his supermarket purchases. The card had been used to buy firelighters of the same type used in the arson attempt. And that, it seems, was sufficient to place him under arrest. The story has a happy ending – Lieutenant Lyons was vindicated when all charges against him were dropped – but only in January 2005, after he had suffered over four months' unnecessary worry and anguish. The moral seems to be that even seemingly innocent data collection modes are accessible by the authorities, and can be used against you in a criminal investigation, building a plausible case for the prosecution despite your innocence.

The philosophy behind this marketing method is certainly intrusive but it remains, to a degree, a matter of choice. Once you are aware of how these stores use the information they gather, you can always refuse to send in your warranty card, turn down the offer of a loyalty or club card and buy with cash to prevent any data being taken up.

However, new 'advances' will soon put an end to this choice. We have already seen in chapter 5 how RFID tags, now being incorporated into clothing, books and almost any other consumer durable, can be used to follow the movements and activity of entire countries. But RFID has other uses, chief among them the amassing of profiling data. In 2003, clothing company Benetton raised a storm of protest when they announced that their 'Sisley' line of clothing would soon have such 'smart tags' embedded in the garment's label. When a purchase was made, the buyer's details would be linked to the item's hidden RFID. Scanners could then read the ID of the person who bought the product at any later date. The advert 'selling' this technology shows a lady entering (not leaving) a shop with the caption 'you know who she is, what she bought, when she bought it, and for how much'. When it appeared that the buyer would neither be informed of the presence of this technology ('imperceptible to the wearer', according to one supplier) nor given the choice to deactivate the transmitter, privacy groups called for a boycott of Benetton products, and the company shelved the trial. In the USA, responding to a public outcry against the technology, Wal-Mart recently cancelled plans to tag its consumer products with RFID chips.

Other companies persisted. Tesco set up a trial of this system where, as soon as anyone picked up a Gillette razor (an often shoplifted item), they were secretly and automatically photographed and filed. Levi Strauss & Co., one of the world's largest clothing manufacturers, confirmed in April 2006 that it had begun testing RFID 'hang tags' on clothing shipped to two Mexican and one US retail outlets. Levi Strauss have stated that they will adhere to guidelines issued by CASPIAN (Consumers Against Supermarket Privacy Invasion and Numbering), which require consumers to be notified of RFID data collection. But with US consumer awareness of RFID at abysmal levels (according to some estimates only 10–20 per cent of the population have actually heard the term RFID, let alone the technology's potential for spying), it may be that even responsible companies are relying on majority customer ignorance to allow the compilation of huge amounts of data on shopping habits and brand preference.

As the chips can be programmed to alert the company each time an individual purchaser enters the store wearing an item containing an RFID tag, government surveillance using 'commercial' surveillance also becomes increasingly possible.

With RFID chips, the line between voluntary and covert surveillance begins to blur, and we are led one more step along the 'no-choice' profiling route, a path which government bureaucracies seem increasingly keen for us to follow. The state employs profiling extensively for a variety of worthwhile causes (e.g. identifying those adolescents most likely to commit suicide), and for less benign analysis of their populations, targeting individuals who, the profiles predict, are potential underground activists against anything from animal experimentation to repressive regimes. And they are fast appreciating the information benefits to be gleaned by bringing all these rapidly proliferating databases, both government and commercial, into one all-encompassing nexus of information.

10

CORRELATION: GETTING IT TOGETHER

The ability of commercial interests to 'profile' customers is mirrored among the bureaucracy, police and security organisations in the profiling of a nation's citizens, using massive computer power to collate a series of pre-existing databases. Such 'dataveillance' is arguably the most worrying aspect of all the many surveillance concerns addressed in this book. It has given the authorities undreamed-of power to synthesise all aspects of a person's life into a single, searchable information sink, where everything from the 'subject's' politics to their preferred method of contraception can be brought on screen with the click of a mouse. A vast amount of formerly private data has become available to thousands of government employees, leading inevitably to a sea-change in the balance of power between the state and the individual.

The term 'dataveillance' was coined by Roger Clarke in the early 1980s and defined as 'a new form of surveillance ... the systematic use of personal data systems in the investigation or monitoring of the actions or communications of one or more persons'.[1]

While physical surveillance is expensive, dataveillance is relatively inexpensive and becoming more so as time goes on. This has allowed a change of emphasis: traditional surveillance with 'boots on the ground' could deal with only a limited number of subjects, and it was rare that a target's every movement and communication was monitored 24 hours a day, every day of the year. By contrast, the massive computing power of today's systems means that whole populations can be watched on an ongoing basis at very little expense. Moreover, the data that accumulates can be mined extensively for patterns and anomalies in a way that was impossible for an earlier generation of spies. Dataveillance has dispensed with field operatives and deals instead with dossiers and what has been termed the 'data shadow' or 'digital persona'. The flesh-and-blood individual is reduced to a binary stream, personality replaced by zeros and ones: to all intents and purposes, an individual *is* the information contained in his or her dossier. And should that information be incorrect, or merely flag up the *possibility* of criminal or terrorist activity, a whole host of unfortunate consequences can ensue.

Dataveillance purports to detect undesirable classes of people before they commit any offence. However, the techniques used to form the profiles (called multivariate correlation and discriminant analysis) have limited applicability, constraints which are often ignored when used by inadequately trained or excessively pressured staff, eager to identify suspects. We are in danger of becoming a 'dossier society', where the computer file is considered a truer representation of reality than the individual himself. In such a context, witch-hunts against 'identified' individuals or groups seem inevitable. 'In its most extreme form (one that Kafka could not anticipate), the accuser could be a poorly understood computer programme.'[2]

Dataveillance can be conveniently divided into 'personal', when an individual has been earlier identified as being of interest, and 'mass', where a large number of people (e.g. a political party or ethnic group) is surveilled so as to detect specific individuals within the group and/or discourage 'inappropriate' behaviour. This is an important distinction which we shall return to later.

In his paper, Roger Clarke lists five major *personal* data-veillance techniques:

1. Integration of data hitherto stored in various locations within a single organisation
2. Screening or authentication of transactions against internal norms
3. Front-end verification of transactions that appear to be exceptional, against data relevant to the matter at hand, and sought from other internal databases or from third parties
4. Front-end audit of individuals who appear to be exceptional, against data related to *other* matters, and sought from other internal databases or from third parties
5. Cross-system enforcement against individuals, where a third party reports that the individual has committed a transgression in his or her relationship with the third party.[3]

Such intrusive power on the part of the authorities is bad enough, but at least here surveillance action is undertaken (or should be) only when some anomaly arises. If I bank a cheque for £3,000 in my current account each month over a period of five years, and then suddenly deposit £1,500,000, that is exceptional and it can at least be argued that such a discrepancy requires further investigation. It would be quite another thing if someone in authority suddenly said 'Let's just check on this account, to see if we can find anything incriminating. In fact ... let's do it to all the bank accounts in the country.' There would be justifiable outrage at this gross intrusion into the nation's private life. And yet, this is exactly what mass data-veillance does – and not just for finances.

Clarke also gives an instructive list of five *mass* dataveillance techniques:

1. Screening or authentication of all transactions, whether or not they appear to be exceptional, against internal norms
2. Front-end verification of all transactions, whether or not they appear to be exceptional, against data relevant to the matter at hand, and sought from other internal databases or from third parties
3. Front-end audit of individuals, whether or not they appear to be exceptional, against data related to *other* matters, and sought from other internal databases or from third parties
4. Single-factor file analysis of all data held or able to be acquired, whether or not they appear to be exceptional, variously involving transaction data compared against a norm, permanent data or other transaction data
5. Profiling, or multi-factor file analysis of all data held or able to be acquired, whether or not they appear to be exceptional, variously involving singular profiling of data held at a point in time, or aggregative profiling of transaction trails over time.

Many of the items are similar to those linked to personal data-veillance, but for one vital phrase. With chilling uniformity, the words 'whether or not they appear to be exceptional' appear in every item. The intrusive analysis, then, is clearly an arbitrary action, carried out 'whether or not they appear to be exceptional'; that is, without 'probable cause' (as the term is used in the US legal system) or any prior grounds for suspicion. This cuts at the very foundations of our legal system. Equally, the organisation conducting mass surveillance begins with a presumption of guilt on the part of at least some of those surveilled, although at the beginning of the exercise it is unknown which ones. The result is a prevailing climate of suspicion.

Despite these and other dangers, the procedure is often hyped as a method of identifying tax and benefit cheats and increasing state revenue. The truth is somewhat different; for example, a 1996 matching exercise by the Australian Taxation Office cost A\$17,000,000, yet failed to find a single case of tax evasion. In another case, out of 2,334 investigated for fraud, just 61 had action taken against them. Presumably the other 2,273 were investigated without due cause, an extremely worrying development.[4]

Data-matching is the direct counterpart to arbitrary investigation without cause or suspicion. It is the technological equivalent of a general warrant on the entire population, no different from police being empowered to enter your home in your absence, search through your papers and take copies of whatever they wish. Were this to be done in person, rather than electronically, there would be a public outcry. But, once again, as in other aspects of our surveillance society, because the search is silent and invisible, we fail to protest against the gross violation of our rights. Dataveillance is far more than computers speaking more efficiently to each other. 'It is the systematic development of a vast multi-faceted database that reaches into every aspect of our lives.'

There are four distinct human rights and privacy dilemmas involved here:

1. Data-matching is based on the premise that everyone is potentially suspect. There is thus an assumption of guilt – the presumption of innocence no longer exists.

2. It breaches the privacy principles held in law throughout the (Western) world, chief among these being the principle that information supplied for one function must not be used for another, unless this is consented to.

3. It encourages the use of a single number system. As we've seen in chapter 4, the dangers inherent in a single number system cannot be over-emphasised. Even without this, data-matching, coupled with data-profiling, creates the effect of a single society-wide computer even if no single master computer exists.

4. The accuracy of the data being matched may be inaccurate or incorrectly logged, leading to flawed identification of a 'suspect'. But once 'flagged' by the system, the onus is on the individual to prove his or her innocence, rather than on the government to prove guilt, turning basic justice on its head. Moreover, when private companies are involved, wrongly 'tagged' customers can easily be blacklisted across the entire industry.

In addition, the sheer scale of dataveillance, with its concomitant data-matching and profiling, must give cause for alarm. The United Kingdom, the European Union and the United States have each already initiated systems whose overarching panoptic gaze will touch every citizen within the Western world.

National Identity Register

We have already seen in chapter 4 that the United Kingdom's national identity card scheme is merely the pretext for the establishment of an enormous database on the entire population of these islands, the National Identity Register. Notwithstanding the government's decision to cancel the building of the giant NIR computer, all aspects of the data will still be instantly accessible via networked systems connecting three existing computer systems: the UK's national insurance, asylum and passport databases. It is the networked nature of the data files, linked to a single identity card number, that is of concern, not the physical location of the data. Even the government's own privacy watchdog, the Information Commissioner's Office (ICO), has stated that its main concerns regarding the identity card scheme 'are largely centred upon the proposed National Identity Register ... the amount of information contained in it, the purposes for which it can be used now and in the future, and who may have access to it and for what purposes'. Again, 'the information potentially to be contained in the National Identity Register is extensive and disproportionate burdens are placed on individuals to keep this up to date. [There are crippling penalties for failure to comply – see pp. 76–7.] The continued relevance of all such particulars once identity has been verified upon enrolment is not clear. For example how does the acquisition of a second home after enrolment (Schedule 1(1)(g)) affect an individual's identity? These, and other such details, seem excessive, not relevant and unnecessarily intrusive.'[5]

The ICO is also concerned with:

1. The large number of organisations and government departments allowed access to the information, including biometric data.

159

2. The limited powers given to the ICO to oversee and/or audit the NIR scheme.

3. The lack of a proper Privacy Impact Assessment to judge the likely effects of such government initiatives.

4. The dangers consequent to any technological or administrative failure of the scheme, which could be disastrous for individual citizens. 'Cases have previously arisen where mistakes of "official identity" have led to loss of liberty.'

Despite these concerns, the Identity Cards Bill passed into law substantially unchanged on 13 March 2006. But it is by no means the only mega-database we will have to contend with. Europe is also keen on data collection.

Europe's mega-databases

The new European 'federal police force', Europol, has set up TECS (The Europol Computer System) which will soon be able to provide full analytical details on criminals and, more controversially, on victims, potential victims, those with 'suspected' criminal contacts and perhaps even witnesses. Data on health and race can also be stored and accessed. The plan is to expand the system so that it can store information on at least 1 million individuals. As the system grows, police officers from every European state will be able to access TECS, with the potential for, say, an officer from France (where data protection laws are relatively lax) to access information on a German citizen (whose nation has the strictest data protection laws) and then sell the information to interested parties. This is particularly pertinent following the recent arrest of a Belgian policeman on suspicion of selling data from the Schengen Information System (SIS) to the Mafia.

The SIS is itself being phased out in favour of a second-generation SIS II which, together with another huge database, the Visa Information System (VIS), has been railroaded through the EU system with little to no democratic input from the European Parliament or anyone else. Ben Hayes of civil liberties group Statewatch spent long hours of painstaking research to delve behind the deliberate shielding of this process from parliamentary scrutiny, and this section draws heavily on his work 'Construction of EU's Big Brother Database Underway'.[6]

The initial SIS was shared at first by the five original signatories to the Schengen Convention (France, Germany, Belgium, Luxembourg and the Netherlands) plus Portugal and Spain, and began operating in those countries in 1995. The Convention had abolished border controls between the signatory nations and had set up the Schengen visa for the temporary entry of non-nationals. The SIS was designed primarily as a database to alert customs, border and police officials within the Schengen area to persons and items deemed undesirable or of interest by one or other of the signatory nations. In this it is similar to the UK Police National Computer (PNC) described earlier, but with important differences. Whereas the PNC holds relatively thorough historical and identification details, including biometrics (fingerprints) which may be data-mined, the original SIS worked on a hit/no hit system and contained only six 'alerts', *viz:*

1. People wanted for arrest and extradition (Article 95)
2. People to be refused entry to the Schengen area
   (Article 96)
3. Missing and dangerous people (Article 97)
4. People wanted to appear in court (Article 98)

5. People to be placed under surveillance (Article 99 – 16,016)

6. Lost and stolen objects (Article 100).

There were already concerns with the SIS, most especially on the vague criteria by which individuals could be marked down for 'discreet surveillance' and 'specific checks', and the lack of access to SIS records to discover if you are among those named on the database – there are numerous grounds for refusing such requests. As Ben Hayes commented, 'If people cannot access their data files, then the "right" to have information corrected or deleted, or to seek compensation, is meaningless.'

Rather than address these concerns, the EU merely compounds them with their 'bigger, brighter' database, stating that the new-generation SIS II will be 'a system that can be expanded progressively with additional functionalities'. Four important new functions have been added, each with such grave ramifications that they are worth analysing in some detail.

1 THE ADDITION OF NEW CATEGORIES OF ALERT

Some of these have already been agreed. Few would quibble with the inclusion of the names and personal information of children who will not be allowed to leave the Schengen area, a precaution against kidnap and cases of parental separation. But another category, 'violent troublemakers', is far less cut and dried, as it can be used to prevent '"protestors" travelling to events in other Schengen countries where there is a "risk" that they may cause disorder'. What price then a mass movement against, say, globalisation (or an unpopular EU treaty), if the authorities, on their own initiative, can brand any individual a possible cause of 'disorder' and effectively quarantine that person (and unlimited others) within their own nation?

2 THE ADDITION OF NEW CATEGORIES OF DATA, INCLUDING 'BIOMETRICS'

From its inception, SIS II has held biometric data in the form of fingerprints and digitised 'passport' photographs. This is especially worrying in view of the EU decision that 'all passport holders, residence permit holders and visa applicants will be photographed and fingerprinted using harmonised technology ... Those EU citizens who do not have passports face biometric profiling in national ID card schemes.' This information throws a whole new light on the UK government's insistence on a mandatory national ID card, which should perhaps now be renamed the pan-national ID card. If the Labour government's ID card project goes through, there is the very strong likelihood that the biometrics of every UK citizen will end up on SIS II, along with those of all other 'harmonised' European populations. We are to be numbered and counted like cattle – and on a Europe-wide basis.

Note, too, that the new 'functionalities' already agreed expressly include 'other biometric data'. This is almost certainly a reference to DNA, and would allow the EU to achieve, by stealth, the organisation's long-desired acquisition of an EU DNA database. Combine this with a previously agreed future biometric search facility for SIS II, and the circle is closed.

In contrast, Article 94(3) of the Schengen Convention expressly limits the personal data held on the original SIS to six basic fields: (a) name/surname, (b) distinguishing features, (c) initial of second forename, (d) date and place of birth, (e) sex and (f) nationality; with four additional police-oriented categories: whether the person is (g) armed or (h) violent, (i) the reason for the report, and (j) the action to be taken.

Without any democratic scrutiny, we will have in place a Europe-wide comprehensive biometric (DNA/fingerprint/photographic) database, with a search facility that will give SIS II the means to engage in data-mining and data-matching. This will allow 'fishing expeditions' across the whole database, based on the assumption that everyone is potentially guilty of whatever crime is under investigation. In addition, new categories of alert and new data fields may be added at will. This pernicious development places the entire population of Europe under constant suspicion. And as if this were not bad enough, the third 'functionality' is custom-built to make matters worse.

3 THE INTERLINKING OF ALERTS

On the face of it, interlinking alerts appears to be a sensible addition to SIS II's capabilities: correlating a car thief with a particular stolen car will undoubtedly help in apprehending more criminals.

But the proposal goes much further than this. When we are told by the EU that the intention is to link 'family members', 'gang members' and '*suspected* gang members', a warning bell should sound in everyone's head. What we have here is the introduction of 'intelligence' into the database equation, and as contemporary history has shown in spades (e.g. the Iraq 'dodgy dossier', the de Menezes shooting), intelligence work is based on a great deal of supposition and can often be incorrect. As Ben Hayes comments, this 'greatly improves the chances of innocent people suffering serious repercussions as a result of being "associated" with criminals (or even suspected criminals) ...'

4 WIDENED ACCESS TO SIS II

Considering the opportunities for misuse of the information, the original SIS allowed a disconcerting number of points of access to the system – around 125,000 different locations where the data could be read. Rather than reduce this number, SIS II allows for a massive increase: the UK and Ireland have joined the new system, as have the ten new EU member states. Moreover, four new user groups have been granted access: (a) vehicle registration authorities, (b) 'Europol', the European police office, (c) 'Eurojust', the EU prosecutions agency, and (d) national and judicial prosecuting authorities. Just as worrying, there is an informal agreement to allow access to SIS II for internal security and external intelligence agencies.

Article 101 of the Schengen Convention *expressly precludes* widened access to SIS. But once again a stealthy, incremental approach, by those intent on imposing increasing levels of surveillance on massive numbers of people, has achieved over a reasonably short time what would never have been granted as a single package. The original SIS was limited to police and immigration checks, but SIS II is a very different sack of potatoes – a dataveillance machine of awesome power able to implement a host of law enforcement and 'security' functions and available to a huge number of organisations.

And there is more. In a flagrant breach of one of data protection's most fundamental principles (that data must only be used for the purpose for which it was collected), another catch-all phrase has been inserted, allowing 'the possibility to give partial access with a purpose different from the original one set out in the alerts'. In essence new users, and new uses for the data held on millions of people (and potentially for the 450 million-strong population of the EU), can be added to SIS II – by Euro-diktat.

America – Total Recall

America, of course, thinks even bigger. In 2003, the Pentagon announced the launch of LifeLog – a research project designed to harvest information about every part of an individual's life, to index the data and make it searchable. 'LifeLog must acquire data to capture both the user's physical experiences in the world and his or her interactions with other entities in the world', according to a release by the Defence Advanced Research Projects Agency (DARPA). All available surveillance data – every telephone call made, email sent, webpage browsed, every magazine, newspaper, TV or radio programme read, watched or listened to – would be added to the database, and combined with GPS surveillance to locate the individual at any given time, audio-visual info to track what he/she saw or did, and biomedical information gleaned from medical databases and implanted monitors. In its briefing paper, DARPA points out that the information could be used to 'trace the threads of an individual's life, to see exactly how a relationship or events developed ... by using a search-engine interface'. In effect, a 'Google' of your entire existence.

As might be expected, such a proposal caused uproar among civil liberties groups who lobbied hard to see an end to the project. Early in 2004 their efforts bore fruit and the Pentagon reluctantly killed off the controversial project, along with similar DARPA schemes such as FutureMap.

However, a second, lower-profile Pentagon project (launched in 2002) escaped unscathed. Total Information Awareness (TIA) was intended 'to capture the "information signature" of people so that the government could track potential terrorists and criminals involved in "low-intensity/low-density" forms of warfare and crime'.[7]

The project was headed by Admiral (retired) John Poindexter, who famously lost his job as National Security Adviser under Ronald Reagan and was convicted of conspiracy, lying to Congress, defrauding the government and destroying evidence in the Iran-Contra scandal. He was later appointed vice-president of Syntek Technologies – a government contractor which had worked with DARPA to develop Genoa, a 'military-grade

Google/Napster' used for instant analysis of electronic data and an integral part of the TIA scheme – before being made director of DARPA's 'Information Awareness Office', after 9/11.

TIA's 'revolutionary technology for ultra-large all-source information repositories' would create a 'virtual, centralised, grand database'. This would track millions of people, collecting as much information about them as possible and employing computer algorithms and human analysis to identify potentially criminal or terrorist activity.

The civil liberties dangers inherent in such a scheme were not lost on the US public. The Pentagon attempted to avert the destruction of the project by renaming it 'Terrorist Information Awareness' – apparently relying on the 'Al Qaeda factor' to help the proposal's acceptability. The rebranding exercise failed, and in September 2003 Congress removed funding for the controversial project and closed the Pentagon's Information Awareness Office, Poindexter having resigned over a month earlier on 12 August 2003.

But the surveillance benefits to government from such schemes are so great that the concept refuses to die. Having tried and failed with both LifeLog and TIA on a nationwide basis, the next move was to downsize the project and, by conducting the surveillance on a state-by-state basis, to obtain the same information by stealth (it would be relatively easy to combine state databases at a later date). Enter MATRIX (Multistate Anti-TeRorism Information eXchange) which, despite using state data, was actually seed-funded by the federal government to the tune of $12 million. Matrix proponents claimed it merely streamlined police access to information about suspects that authorities have long been able to get from disparate sources. But the truth was somewhat darker: in 2003, a top Florida police official (Florida's Department of Law Enforcement spearheaded the Matrix programme) told the *Washington Post* that the project was so powerful it was 'scary' and that 'it could be abused. I mean, I can call up everything about you, your pictures and pictures of your neighbors.'[8]

Documents obtained by the American Civil Liberties Union (ACLU) indicate that it could also be made to sift through vast stores of Americans' personal data and proactively finger crime and terrorism suspects. A private company, Seisint Inc. of Boca Raton, Florida was heavily involved and had been contracted to combine its vast databases on millions of individuals with state records, allowing details of the property, boats and internet domains that citizens owned to be accessed, along with their address history, utility connections, bankruptcies, liens and business filings. Despite the 'state-run' façade, federal government was to have access via the FBI and the Department of Homeland Security. And in a further link with the federal government, Seisint Inc. was found to have former federal law enforcement officials on its staff, including managing director Brian Stafford, former head of the Secret Service. Documents obtained by the ACLU and the Electronic Privacy Information Centre boasted of Matrix's ability to rapidly display data, together with pictures of individuals on file, and perform analysis: 'The user can easily see relationships between people, places and things that were previously impossible to discern … With minimal input and the push of a button, witnesses, associates, relatives and suspects can be identified and located.'

Civil liberties groups were outraged and led a major campaign to have Matrix shut down. 'This is the state version of TIA,' said Barry Steinhardt, head of ACLU's technology and liberty programme, '… a major program with very large ambitions, and it needs to be publicly examined. We shouldn't be forced to read tea leaves,' he added. 'Who's really pulling the strings and funding the program and creating its contours,' Steinhardt said, 'are answers only hinted at so far.'

Many Americans took up the protest and on 15 April 2005, two years after the project was begun, a press release issued by the Florida Department of Law Enforcement announced the programme's shutdown due to lack of federal funding.

But even before Matrix was declared dead, Son of Matrix was born in the Sunshine State of Florida. In a 12 April call for information, three days before Matrix was officially abandoned, law enforcement officials called on technology firms to set out their newest wares, envisioning a 'Matrix II' that would include more types of data than the original, including financial and insurance records. Mark Zadra, chief of Florida's Office of Statewide Intelligence, said the state wanted to rebuild the system and hoped other states would join. 'Once we do the competitive procurement process and if we see there is an easy way to share information with other states, other states may want to take advantage of [it].' Other arms of government have taken a less obvious approach to resuscitating Matrix. In a by-now familiar stealth tactic, they have concentrated on developing components of the system that can easily be 'bolted' together, connected at a distance to perform the same function. Matrix dispersed is, they hope, below the radar of media and public perception. And so far, they've been proved right.

The lack of interest in dispersed systems points up a curious fact about the level of public concern and awareness of surveillance systems: the extraordinary compliance that whole nations evince as traditional freedoms melt away and the surveillance net is gradually tightened around society. But then, for many people this is hardly an issue. We have been assimilated into the surveillance collective all unknowing, and hardly realise or acknowledge our subservience. How has this come about?

11

ENSURING ACQUIESCENCE:
THE CARROT AND THE STICK

The carrot

We hear much about the 'Orwellian' dynamic in our society, but in truth the changes we are witnessing owe more to Huxley's *Brave New World* than anything found in *Nineteen Eighty-four*. Instead of repressive tyrants and omnipresent intrusive technology we are in the midst of a process of mass pacification. Computers and technology have been designed to be user-friendly – all the hard-to-understand jargon, all the sharp edges have been smoothed away. Technology is our friend, non-judgmental and ever-present and eventually ... invisible. The danger of a ubiquitous technological environment was seen as long ago as 1991, when Mark Weiser, chief technologist of the Xerox Palo Alto Research Center (PARC), pointed out that 'the most profound technologies are those that disappear. They weave themselves into the fabric of everyday life until they are indistinguishable from it.'[1]

This ubiquitous computing (or ubicomp), known in Europe as ambient intelligence (AmI), is already well advanced, with plans for ultra-convenient RFID personal biometric monitors woven into clothing to act as a cue for lighting and heating within the home, altering our personal environment continuously and without our conscious awareness. Refrigerators that

171

monitor (via RFID again) our food stocks and automatically order replacements from the supermarket when we run low form another frequently mentioned example of the ubicomp environment.

We are developing a childlike dependence on technology: it informs us, entertains us, cooks our food, even gives us directions when driving. Our mobile phones keep us connected to friends and family, credit cards transfer funds for goods and services in a fraction of a second. We know our laptop like an intimate friend, one to whom we are happy to confide our hidden interests and passions. But beyond the slick technology is a darker reality. Our computer is less a friend than a gossip, its console less a TV screen than a one-way mirror. We see only the reflections of our own commands appearing on the screen – we do not observe the myriad individuals and organisations who are collecting our every keystroke and using it to record, analyse and sell on to others everything we buy, our sexual preferences, what our political affiliations are, and a host of other private transactions.

Intimacy and 'bonding' with the machine lowers our resistance, salves our suspicion and lulls us into a sense of false security. Each day we unwittingly divulge more and more about ourselves to our electronic friend, forgetting that we are no longer playing with individual gadgets – we are dealing with an overarching technological umbrella, and the complex mass of information we allow to be placed under this umbrella 'will be passed on endlessly, to be configured and reconfigured, sold, resold, and redirected in a thousand ingenious ways'.[2]

But note: there is no coercion here. We are all so cosy with technology that, with no thought, we routinely hand over enormous amounts of personal info, or subscribe to a road toll system that may cut a minute or two off our daily travel time, but will at the same time ensure that, 24/7 and year-round, no confidential data we possess, no journey we make, will escape technology's all-seeing eye. If we choose to accept the benefits of these technologies without considering their attendant risks, then we are assuming that the possibility of creeping government repression – leading ultimately to the establishment of a controlled society – is non-existent. This flies in the face of all historical precedent; given human nature and the desire of individuals and groups for dominance, such an assumption is a reckless betrayal of all our society's freedoms. And for what? More convenient shopping and a shorter delay at the toll booth?

On the rare occasions that mass protest does erupt, the wise government espouses *compromise*, making minor changes, or even ostentatiously shelving a large part of the programme (intending to introduce it in stages, by stealth, later – see for example chapter 14, p. 223ff). This normally has the effect of neutralising opposition. In a liberal democracy people feel uncomfortable holding 'extreme' views, even on such topics as basic freedoms, and if the other side offers 'concessions', they feel duty-bound to reciprocate. A sham compromise effectively disarms resistance and allows repressive legislation to creep, stage by stage, over our liberties.

The stick

When cosmetic changes and compromise are insufficient, the authorities promote a climate of fear and loathing; ID cards have been in turn a cure for benefit scroungers, illegal immigrants, and terrorists. This latter grouping has been the most useful as, although we may loathe benefit scroungers, we actively fear terrorists, a shadowy grouping who have the power to take away our health and life without warning. The fight against this nemesis has been given an elevated status: the 'war on terror'. Today the term is a little out of fashion, and while President George W. Bush still mentions the WoT, Prime Minister Gordon Brown has apparently forbidden the phrase. But then again, it has served its purpose.

If we step back and view the broad canvas of events over the past decade, it is obvious that 11 September 2001 was the tipping point for all matters of a surveillance nature. There had, of course, been surveillance before this date: CCTV had been in operation for some 25 years, and wire-tapping and mail intercepts were not unknown. But post-9/11 it is obvious that an absolute deluge of legislation and surveillance has been unleashed on the nations of Western Europe and the United States. An editorial in *Surveillance & Society* succinctly describes events:

> Suddenly, during 2001, the steady increase in surveillance received a boost from a world event. September 11 prompted widespread international concern for security in the face of global terrorism ... Already existing surveillance was reinforced at crucial points, with the promise of more to come. Many countries rapidly passed laws permitting unprecedented levels of policing and intelligence surveillance, which in turn draws upon other sources such as consumer records.[3]

The attack on the Twin Towers of the World Trade Centre is the *causa causans*, the fount and origin of the term 'war on terror', and the fundamental justification for those who claim we face so grave a situation that we must be prepared to give up many of our basic freedoms in order to live in reasonable security. It behoves us, therefore, to look very closely at the events of 9/11 and to decide if we really are in such great danger as some would have us believe, or if the threat has been exaggerated in order to serve another agenda.

In chapter 5 we looked at the idea of defining the 'topography of the argument' so as to steal a march on rival arguments: *progressive* teaching, wind *farms* and the like. Now we have the '*war* on terror'. It is instructive to ask whether the draconian measures implemented since 9/11 would have received such an easy passage had the president announced a 'campaign against terror', or an 'anti-terror initiative'. The word 'war' successfully defines the topography of the argument in favour of the hawks and those advocating extreme measures, because a war *demands* extreme measures.

The immediate parallels with the threat of Islamic extremism, at least for the United Kingdom, must lie with the IRA action of the last half of the 20th century. Note that this conflict was never graced with the title 'war'; on the contrary, because successive UK governments did not wish to emphasise the level and consequences of sectarian dissension in the province, the conflict was 'the Troubles' – a phrase that, even now, serves to defuse the impact of the murders, bombings and religious violence that Northern Ireland suffered for more than 25 years.

IRA activity led to innumerable deaths and mutilations. According to the book *Lost Lives*, up to 2004 the IRA were responsible for 1,781 deaths,[4] while around 20,000 were injured (6,000 of them British Army, UDR or RUC personnel and up to 14,000 civilians).[5] The paramilitaries killed Lord Mountbatten, a cousin of the Queen, the Conservative MP Airey Neave, and they attempted to kill the then prime minister Margaret Thatcher and most of her Cabinet in the Brighton bombing of 12 October 1984. Against this, in the UK the jihadists have managed the 7/7 tube and bus bombing with a death toll of 52, and a failed bombing fourteen days later. And yet the IRA attacks were 'Troubles' which did not even lead to the introduction of additional passport restrictions on citizens of the Irish Republic, and whose impact on the freedoms of the British people (internment in Northern Ireland excepted) was minimal. In contrast, a single successful bombing has led to Britain acting as a willing ally to the 'war on terror's' main protagonist, the USA. What lies behind this perceptual dichotomy that we are invited – or rather, instructed – to accept?

It is not that the threat of Islamic extremism is non-existent; it is the disproportionate response, the asymmetrical manner in which we are asked to perceive the threat, and the blatant over-reaction in terms of legislation and deployment of surveillance technology, that gives cause for concern. In terms of actual damage and deaths, the jihadists have not demonstrated one hundredth of the destructive potential of the IRA. Why, then, should a terrorist threat of low intensity result in an exponential rise in draconian legislation and intrusive surveillance powers? Is this merely a political panic attack, or are we looking at an orchestrated dismantling of our freedoms?

The politicians, of course, insist it is neither of these alternatives. The justification lies not in terrorist activity seen to date in the UK, but in the catastrophic fact of the attack on the World Trade Centre. If the jihadists are able and willing to mount attacks on this scale, resulting in the collapse of enormous structures with huge loss of life, then – so the argument goes – we are dealing with a threat level well outside of that posed by the IRA, UDA, ETA, or any of the many extremist groups that currently populate our planet. And in the face of such a challenge, all the many recent restrictions and intrusions on our freedom are, they argue, necessary for our own good.

Time and again, then, we come back to 9/11 as the pivotal moment, the raison d'être, for the exponential growth in the most repressive aspects of the surveillance society. ID cards, centralised databases, RFID tagging, electronic surveillance and the rest, all are presently necessary to protect us against the jihadists, and the reason the jihadists are to be feared is 9/11.

If this is so, we should certainly look very closely at the circumstances of this iconic attack on Western civilisation.

World Trade Centre 7 and the 'prophetic' BBC

There are already a huge number of books, articles and TV
programmes concerning the attack on the Twin Towers, and it
is not the purpose of this work to enumerate a minute-by-
minute account of the disaster. Nor to apportion blame. Indeed,
looking too closely at the minutiae of such events is sometimes
counter-productive; we have had, for example, numerous 'human
interest' TV programmes on 9/11, the plight of individuals, the
dangers facing fire crews etc, but too few on the accusations
and counter-accusations that have made the attack so prob-
lematical. There is, however, one part of 9/11 that must give
any thinking person pause: not the destruction of the twin towers
(World Trade Centre 1 and 2), but the little-reported collapse
of World Trade Centre 7, more than seven hours *after* the first of
the Twin Towers came down. And the BBC's ability to cover
its destruction 26 minutes before it actually occurred.

A new Pearl Harbor?

For more than 50 years controversy has raged around the
Japanese attack on the US naval base of Pearl Harbor in 1941
– was it, as Franklin D. Roosevelt said, a 'day of infamy' when
Japanese planes appeared out of a clear blue sky and brought
death and destruction to an unsuspecting American Pacific Fleet?
Or did the American government have advance warning of the
planned attack, and choose to allow an outrage to occur in
order to awaken an isolationist American public to the dangers

of fascist Germany and a Japan with grandiose imperial pretensions?

In *Infamy: Pearl Harbor and its Aftermath*, Pulitzer Prize-winning journalist John Toland revealed compelling evidence that President Roosevelt had foreknowledge of the event, yet chose to do nothing.[6] Robert Stinnett, in his book *Day Of Deceit*, presents massive evidence that Roosevelt intended to goad the Japanese into an overt attack.[7] Indeed, in the Vacant Seas order, Roosevelt had cleared both civilian and naval shipping away from the Japanese fleet's attack route, in order to aid the enemy's undetected approach to within striking distance of Pearl Harbor. The release of former secret files from the US Navy has shown that the US had broken the Japanese Navy's codes and knew exactly where and when the attack would take place. The more valuable US ships such as aircraft carriers were ordered out of Pearl to other locations. Tellingly, 69 of the 74 Navy intelligence summaries delivered to President Roosevelt in the two weeks prior to the attack have been 'lost'.[8]

In sum, the Pearl Harbor 'let it happen' scenario is at least plausible, and given the undoubted isolationist feeling among the US public, a good argument can be made that it was, despite the underhand way in which it was carried out, absolutely essential to the final victory over fascism.

The parallels between the situation facing President Roosevelt in 1940 and that confronting the Bush administration at the beginning of the 21st century are compelling. The Taliban and their terrorist training camps had been identified as a clear threat to United States interests, just as Nazi Germany and an imperially-minded Japan had been over 50 years earlier. And despite what was seen, by the respective US administrations at least, as a pressing need to destroy their enemy before they gained in strength, in both cases the American public were steadfastly against foreign military adventures. Roosevelt's answer, as we know from recently declassified correspondence, was to provoke Japan into making the first overt act of aggression, so justifying a military response and letting the president off the hook of his electoral promise not to send American boys to fight abroad unless the US were attacked. The breaking of the Japanese codes, the failure to warn Pearl Harbor, the movement of strategically important vessels, the Vacant Seas policy, all make it highly likely that the president of the United States took the decision to sacrifice the men and women at Pearl Harbor in order to prevent an even greater catastrophic loss of life and geopolitical influence in the future. Captain Joseph J. Rochefort was head of the Navy's Mid-Pacific Radio Intelligence Network before and during the Pearl Harbor attack. In his oral history for the US Naval Institute, he put the case for allowing the attack to go ahead with characteristic succinctness: 'It was', he said, 'a pretty cheap price to pay for unifying the country.'[9]

And by a strange coincidence, exactly twelve months before the 9/11 attacks a major American 'neo-con' think tank cited 'another Pearl Harbor' as the quickest means of bringing about the transformation of American military and geopolitical strength. The Project for a New American Century (PNAC) was founded in 1996 to promote an agenda for strengthening America's position and influence in the world. In September 2000 it published *Rebuilding America's Defenses: Strategy, Forces and Resources for a New Century*, in which it claimed that '... the process of transformation [in American strategy and forces], even if it brings revolutionary change, is likely to be a long one, absent some catastrophic and catalyzing event – like a new Pearl Harbor.'[10]

This comment does not, as some have insisted, reveal a plot to launch 9/11. But it does show that the value of a 'new Pearl

Harbor' in bringing about transformational change was acknowledged by PNAC. Of interest, too, is the fact that a significant number of PNAC's founders and signers are working for, or have worked for, the Bush administration, including Dick Cheney, Richard Armitage, Paul Wolfowitz and Donald Rumsfeld.

This is far from proving that the Bush administration instigated a 'new Pearl Harbor' in order to allow major changes in US foreign and domestic policy. And yet the idea is not perhaps as incredible as it might at first appear – the US government has certainly considered similar ideas at least once before. A fifteen-page US government Top Secret document dated 13 March 1962 and entitled *Chairman, Joint Chiefs of Staff, Justification for US Military Intervention in Cuba* detailed, among other deceptions, a number of ways that attacks on American soil *by US operatives* could be used to stir up national indignation and act as a pretext for the invasion of communist Cuba. Among the suggestions in what has become known as Operation Northwoods was using drone planes to simulate an attack on an American passenger aeroplane. Below are two extracts from this document:

> It is possible to create an incident which will demonstrate convincingly that a Cuban aircraft has attacked and shot down a chartered civil airliner en route from the United States ...

> We could develop a Communist Cuba terror campaign in the Miami area, in other Florida cities and even in Washington ... We could sink a boatload of Cubans en route to Florida (real or simulated). We could foster attempts on lives of Cuban refugees in the United States even to the extent of wounding in instances to be widely publicized. Exploding a few plastic bombs in carefully chosen spots, the arrest of Cuban agents and the release

of prepared documents substantiating Cuban involvement also would be helpful in projecting the idea of an irresponsible [Cuban] government.[11]

To sum up, it seems likely that:

1. Pearl Harbor was a 'managed event', used as a means of uniting the nation in an acceptance that American foreign policy should change.
2. Not only had similar plans been considered in 1962 (despite the risk of loss of life to American citizens in 'Homeland America'), but that
3. the value of such a 'new Pearl Harbor' to rapidly 'transforming' American geopolitical perceptions had been explicitly acknowledged as late as September 2000 by a group (PNAC) which would contribute major players to the Bush administration.

This is emphatically NOT a smoking gun. But it does bring a note of caution to the proceedings; we should take nothing for granted, and should look at the events surrounding the attack on the World Trade Centre with unbiased eyes, refusing to pass over or omit awkward facts.

A possible scenario would see the US intelligence services aware of the impending jihadist attack, allowing it to go ahead and, knowing the targets involved well ahead of the event, using this lead time to enhance the destructiveness of the attack, making it a visual spectacle that would burn itself into the nation's psyche and conjure up an unstoppable demand for retribution. And indeed, there are many anomalies in the World Trade Centre/Pentagon attacks, deeply unsettling questions that remain unanswered while the mass media continue to uncritically regurgitate the official version.

Of all the many anomalies, none is so strange and compelling as the collapse of 7 World Trade Centre. Rather than get bogged down in a detailed overview of the attacks on the Twin Towers and the Pentagon, this discussion will concentrate solely on 7 WTC. There are many advantages to this, not least of which is the bewildering complexity of the full story. By focussing on 7 WTC, we can look at a manageable event and come to some valid conclusions that should be applicable to the attack as a whole. 7 WTC is interesting for two main facts which no one disputes:

1. 7 WTC collapsed without any active terrorist involvement, six hours after the main attack on 1 and 2 WTC (the Twin Towers).
2. The BBC announced the collapse of this building 26 minutes before it fell.

The official version of 7 WTC's destruction is that debris from the fall of 1 and 2 WTC weakened the building, and ignited fires which led to its eventual collapse. The map opposite shows the relative positions of the seven separate World Trade Centre buildings that were dispersed across World Trade Centre Plaza. As is obvious, of all the buildings, 7 WTC lies furthest from the Twin Towers (1 and 2 WTC) whose eventual downfall generated so much controversy. It might therefore reasonably be expected to receive far less damage than those buildings closer to the collapse. And while this protection-by-distance might well be mitigated by the fact that 7 WTC is the tallest of the remaining buildings, and therefore perhaps more vulnerable in its higher storeys to damage from the destruction of 1 and 2 WTC, the nature of the collapse (for all practical purposes, the Twin Towers fell within their own footprint) would mean that the majority of any debris ejected would originate from the base of the collapsed buildings. If this is so, then, looking at the map below, it is obvious that 6 and 5 WTC would act as shields for 7 WTC. And in fact 5 and 6 WTC did suffer extensive damage, but did not collapse. By contrast, 7 WTC sustained far less damage, implying that the 'shield effect' hypothesis is substantially correct. And yet it, alone of all the other WTC buildings, did collapse.[12]

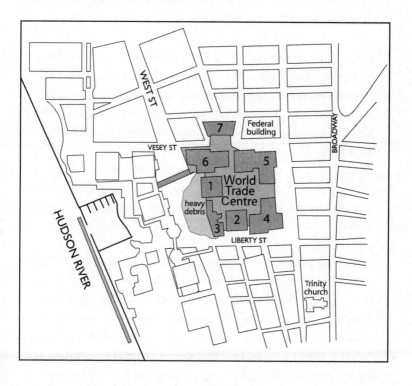

It is valid to ask why this particular building went down, and there are no easy answers. This conflicts with an eyewitness interview conducted by Jason Bermas with Barry Jennings, the deputy director of the Emergency Services Department of the New York

City Housing Authority. According to Jennings, not long after 1 WTC had been hit by an aircraft, but *before* the attack on 2 WTC, he escorted Mr Hess, one of Mayor Rudy Giuliani's highest-ranking appointed officials, to the Office of Emergency Management (OEM) on 7 WTC's 23rd floor. This office was the command bunker where any emergency in the WTC area was to be handled, and was staffed by US security personnel. What he found astounded him: the entire emergency headquarters had been abandoned. This is his story:

> Upon arriving into the OEM EOC we noticed that everybody had gone. I saw coffee that was on the desk, still – smoke was still coming off the coffee, I saw – I saw uh, half eaten sandwiches. And I called several individuals, one individual told me that, that um, 'to leave, and leave right away' ... We subsequently went to the stairwell and we were going down the stairs. When we reached the 8th uh, the 6th floor, the landing that we were standing on gave way. There was an explosion and the landing gave way. And I was left there hanging. I had to walk back up to the 8th floor. After getting to the 8th floor everything was dark.
>
> I'm just confused about one thing, and one thing only. Why WTC 7 went down in the first place? I'm very confused about that. I know what I heard. I heard explosions. The explanation I got was that it was the fuel oil tank. I'm an old boiler guy. If it was a fuel oil tank it would have been one side of the building. When I got to that lobby, the lobby was totally destroyed. It looked like King Kong had came through it and stepped on it. And I – it was so destroyed I didn't know where I was. It was so destroyed they had to take me out through a hole in the wall, a makeshift hole that I believe the fire depot made to get me out.[13]

Let us be clear about this. A well-respected, credible witness is stating that he was in the 7 WTC building and that there was a devastating explosion *before* the second of the Twin Towers was even hit by an aircraft, and long before either 1 or 2 WTC came down (this latter event being the supposed cause of the fires and damage that made 7 WTC fall). Just as worryingly, the explosion seems to have been planned, as all the OEM staff had vacated the building and Mr Jennings was told by an unnamed source to flee WTC, 'to leave, and leave right away'. And this was no small explosion: it wiped out the entire lobby and (contrary to official claims) caused many deaths too. Equally concerning, if this event was planned – and taking Barry Jennings' testimony at face value it is very difficult to see how it was not – it could not have been put into effect in the few minutes that had elapsed since the first aeroplane struck the first tower. Such a plan called for prior knowledge of the attack hours, even days, before the event.

The BBC announcement – clairvoyance, chance or something else?

From the time of the first attack on 11 September, the BBC newsreaders, like most of the world's media, had been providing a constant stream of updates on the unprecedented situation in New York.

At 21.54 London time on 11 September 2001, a BBC newsreader made the sombre announcement that the Salomon Brothers building (another name for 7 WTC) had collapsed:

Now more on the latest building collapse in New York. You might have heard a few moments ago we were talking about the Salomon Brothers building collapsing, and indeed it has.

185

Apparently that was only a few hundred yards away from where the World Trade Centre towers were. And it seems this was not the result of a new attack, it was because the building has been weakened during this morning's attack.

There was just one problem with this news: it was wrong. Or rather, it was a little ahead of time. 7 WTC was still standing when the broadcast was made – it did not collapse until 26 minutes later, at 22.20 London time.

As if to compound the error, the London anchorman then handed over to his New York colleague Jane Standley, who carried on the report of the collapse apparently unaware that the 7 WTC building could still be seen on the right of the screen, behind her left shoulder. This point needs to be emphasised: the visual evidence here is absolutely irrefutable. As the BBC reporter confirms the destruction of 7 WTC it stands as large as life on the screen behind her. And, enhancing the *Alice in Wonderland* nature of the report, as Ms Standley continues to comment on this new 'collapse', a strap line appears across the lower half of the screen confirming the news: 'The 47-storey Salomon Brothers building close to the World Trade Centre has also collapsed.'

But there is more. At around 22.15, as Jane Standley continues to hold forth on the non-existent collapse (with 7 WTC still standing proudly behind her), a very strange thing happens. Had this broadcast conversation continued for a further five minutes (and there was no sign of it winding down), we would have been treated to the spectacle of 7 WTC collapsing for real, on air, behind Ms Standley. But, *mirabile dictu,* at this crucial moment, just five minutes before the actual collapse, the image of Jane Standley begins to break up and the BBC loses the feed and the picture from New York.

BBC News 24 also broadcast the news that 7 WTC had collapsed, with a corroborative time stamp on their broadcast to confirm, without fear of contradiction, that the BBC was somehow aware of the destruction of 7 WTC around half an hour before it went down.[14]

Richard Porter, the head of news at BBC World, offered this explanation for these astonishing events:

1. We're not part of a conspiracy. Nobody told us what to say or do on September 11th. We didn't get told in advance that buildings were going to fall down. We didn't receive press releases or scripts in advance of events happening.

2. In the chaos and confusion of the day, I'm quite sure we said things which turned out to be untrue or inaccurate – but at the time were based on the best information we had. We did what we always did – sourced our reports, used qualifying words like 'apparently' or 'it's reported' or 'we're hearing' and constantly tried to check and double check the information we were receiving.

3. Our reporter Jane Standley was in New York on the day of the attacks, and like everyone who was there, has the events seared on her mind. I've spoken to her today and unsurprisingly, she doesn't remember minute-by-minute what she said or did – like everybody else that day she was trying to make sense of what she was seeing; what she was being told; and what was being told to her by colleagues in London who were monitoring feeds and wires services.

4. We no longer have the original tapes of our 9/11 coverage (for reasons of cock-up, not conspiracy). So if someone

has got a recording of our output, I'd love to get hold of it. We do have the tapes for our sister channel News 24, but they don't help clear up the issue one way or another.

5. If we reported the building had collapsed before it had done so, it would have been an error – no more than that.

This is, with the greatest respect, simply not good enough. Much of Mr Porter's carefully worded comments contradict one another; others are plainly untrue:

1. *We didn't get told in advance that buildings were going to fall down.* No one is accusing the BBC of this. But it is obvious that the BBC was told in advance that a building *had fallen* down. This is a crucial point. Someone told the BBC that 7 WTC had collapsed. Who had foreknowledge of this event? The BBC doesn't say.

2. Elsewhere in the statement Mr Porter admits that their news output (in line with other news services) was based on incoming information from a variety of sources. He states that BBC colleagues in London *were monitoring feeds and wires services* and that *we did what we always did – sourced our reports* and *constantly tried to check and double check the information we were receiving.* If that is the case, then why did they not pick up on the fact that the story was blatantly untrue? More importantly, there should be a record at the BBC of the source of the '7 WTC collapse' story. Who made this claim? Which agency

fed this information through to BBC News – was it Reuters? Voice of America? Associated Press? Knowing the source of the information would allow us to move one step back along the chain of responsibility, and perhaps come to a clearer judgement on the motivation behind the story.

3. [We] *used qualifying words like 'apparently' or 'it's reported' or 'we're hearing'*. This is simply not true. As one commentator noted:

> In the most important final 7 minutes and 15 seconds of the said segment the words 'apparently', 'it's reported' or 'we're hearing' are not used in the context of building 7, viz.:
> 'Now more on the latest building collapse in New York ... the Salomon Brothers Building collapse ... and indeed it has.'
> 'What can you tell us about the Salomon Building and its collapse?'
> 'When it collapsed.'
> [Ticker] – 'The 47-storey Salomon Brothers building close to the World Trade Centre has also collapsed.'

This same commentator also asks: 'Who is responsible for the newsroom in-desk and floor prompters being used by the news presenter? Who is responsible for the news report on the bottom screen news ticker? Who is responsible as the newsroom floor source for giving these people information? What is the complete list of editors and journalists responsible for this program on said day?' None of this information has been vouchsafed by the BBC.

4. *We no longer have the original tapes of our 9/11 coverage.* This statement beggars belief, and brings to mind other convenient document misplacements, like the Belgrano incident's missing submarine logs. Such a loss appears even less likely in the face of BBC policy which states:

> Ref No. Policy Area/Policy Statement 01 Components to be Retained 01-01

> The following components to be retained:

> • Two broadcast standard copies of all transmitted/ published TV, radio and BBCi output – one to be stored on a separate site as a master
> • One browse-quality version for research purposes, to protect the broadcast material.[15]

5. *In the chaos and confusion of the day, I'm quite sure we said things which turned out to be untrue or inaccurate – but at the time were based on the best information we had.* This is exactly the point: in the chaos and confusion the BBC *omits* all qualifiers such as 'apparently' or 'we've unconfirmed reports that …' and gives the correct name of the building, the precise number of floors in that building (47), the explanation of the collapse (that 7 WTC was weakened by damage from the collapse of 1 and 2 WTC), and the Corporation even knows that the building was apparently empty. This is no throw-away remark or rumour that somehow took on the robe of truth; this is detailed, accurate data. Where did this information originate? It is all very unsettling. As one

commentator notes, this is 'some pretty precise reporting for a day of chaos when everyone was "trying to make sense of what they were seeing ..."'

6. *If we reported the building had collapsed before it had done so, it would have been an error – no more than that.* But it is much more than that – it was an error that turned out to be true. It was prescient. The likelihood that the BBC, or anyone else, would suddenly decide, *de novo*, that another building would collapse – no, more, that it *had* collapsed – when the only buildings that had fallen so far were those struck by large passenger jets, has to be vanishingly small. And yet someone does make up this incredible tale, the BBC reports it as fact, and 26 minutes later, the incredible occurs. To call it an 'error' does not even come close. We need to know the originator of this story, the man or woman who can foretell the future with such impressive accuracy. The BBC must have the name of this person or organisation – the Corporation has a moral obligation to bring this information into the public domain.

The BBC's disingenuous approach to what must be regarded as a highly suspicious series of events has satisfied no one. A posting on the net encapsulates the feelings of anger and frustration felt by many:

You lose footage of one of the most important days in modern history ... (Good job! That way no one can 'prove' anything that day ...) Out of all the surrounding buildings that suffered massive damage – WTC 3, 4, 5, 6 – and assorted others that suffered minor damage (among them, WTC 7 – Salomon Brothers Building), the BBC – by merely a mistake and in confusion –

picked exactly the right one that was going to fall – (Good job!) Hey, the BBC is incompetent – they lose tapes AND they claim buildings fall that haven't – but what LUCK! They hit the lottery! What a 'lucky guess', huh? BBC should go to Vegas, with those odds – you'd be rich. BBC is not part of the conspiracy – but you are just a bunch of pathetic dupes. You capture the biggest smoking gun in history ... and your response is ... to call yourselves incompetent and go play 'blind/deaf/dumb monkey' on your public. Good job, Guys!![16]

Despite the obvious parallels between Pearl Harbor and 9/11, one huge disparity remains. While Pearl Harbor resulted in military action abroad, very little change occurred within mainland America itself. With the exception of the arguably unconstitutional internment of US citizens of Japanese origin, the freedoms and rights of the American people were left largely unscathed by World War II. Nor were the rights of other nations materially affected by the Japanese aggression against the United States. Not so with the 'war on terror' which, we have been told with breathtaking arrogance, 'is different from any other war in history'.[17] The attack on the World Trade Centre which precipitated the 'war on terror' has led not only to the invasion of two sovereign states, Afghanistan and Iraq, but to a raft of controlling and repressive legislation (most of it issued in the form of secondary legislation) in both the USA and the United Kingdom, and latterly in many of the EU nations as well, and to intrusive and unnecessary surveillance on an unprecedented scale.

Inevitable war

There is an added danger. While the idea of 'pre-emptive strike' is derided as cowardly and base when it is delivered by the

Japanese on America, the Bush administration (and its UK ally New Labour) appear to have embraced the concept with both hands – if America and friends are doing the striking. Iraq is the example par excellence of this, with 'coalition troops' deployed pre-emptively to prevent the development or use of 'weapons of mass destruction' and to sever links between Al Qaeda and Iraq – both of which motives turned out to be illusory.

But this disastrous symbol of American neo-con philosophy has done nothing to dampen that country's enthusiasm for first-strike action. Iraq is simply the most prominent example of a worrying malaise that is creeping by stealth into the Western democracies – pre-emptive politics and theories of inevitability. Several academics have pointed out that recent statements by politicians have continually stressed the inevitability of disaster; we are told on a regular basis that terrorist attacks are not merely possible, but unstoppable. In May 2002, FBI Director Robert Mueller announced that more suicide bombings in the USA were 'inevitable ... We will not be able to stop it. It's something we all live with.' Vice President Cheney and Donald Rumsfeld both repeatedly used the phrase 'Not a question of if, but when' during several television interviews, as did Tom Ridge, the first Homeland Security Director. Note that very little detail is given, even such obvious parameters as the timescale of these inevitable happenings. Few would argue that a terrorist attack will probably occur sometime in the next ten years, but the rhetorical nature of the repeated emphasis on 'inevitable attack', especially when screened repeatedly via non-critical media, gives the population an impression of predetermined, imminent, repeated attacks about which 'something must be done'. Moreover, much of the evidence upon which these sloganeering statements are made is veiled beneath classified documents that are, by definition, completely unavailable to public scrutiny.

What remains is a faith-based form of politics in which a

political elite claims to be in possession of facts denied the ordinary citizen, who must accept whatever pre-emptive action that elite deems necessary, purely on the basis of trust. What is worrying, as academics Greg Elmer and Andy Opel have pointed out, is that although rarely-read government policy documents offer less strident analyses of these events, 'public statements by a host of public officials, broadcast repeatedly as sound bites, describe a stark, inevitable future of unending terror threats. The contradictions between the written documents and the public statements suggest a wilful attempt to harness the immediacy (and uniformity) of ... news outlets to distribute and maintain an atmosphere of fear and emotion.'[18] And, it might be added, to encourage acquiescence to both foreign pre-emptive strikes and national legislation further restricting personal freedoms.

Given these developments, historical precedent, and the unanswered questions surrounding the World Trade Centre attack – the event which introduced and ostensibly legitimised these unwelcome extensions of state power – we have excellent grounds for suspecting that events may well be being manipulated by groups intent on securing an even firmer grip on power and influence. What laws remain to protect our freedoms, and what can we do to resist further encroachment?

Part 3

DO WE NEED IT – DO WE WANT IT?

Never doubt that a small group of thoughtful, committed citizens can change the world. Indeed, it is the only thing that ever has.
Margaret Mead, anthropologist

12

PROTECTING AUTONOMY

Only 30 years ago, privacy in its broadest sense was acknowledged as a key indicator of the strength of a democracy. In 1975, a ruling of the Californian Supreme Court declared:

> The right of privacy is the right to be left alone. It is a fundamental and compelling interest. It protects our homes, our families, our thoughts, our emotions, our expressions, our personalities, our freedom of communion and our freedom to associate with whom we choose. It prevents government and business interests from collecting and stockpiling unnecessary information about us, and from misusing information gathered for one purpose in order to serve other purposes or embarrass us.

That high position has gradually eroded over the past three decades, until now many of the freedoms of privacy have been seriously curtailed. We have seen how CCTV networks can be set up with little regard to privacy or planning, how cross-matching of data (dataveillance) and export of information offshore proceeds almost unchecked, how emails and mobile phone conversations are open to scrutiny on the flimsiest of pretexts, or none at all. Virtually all domestic law includes exemptions for national security. What safeguards, if any, remain to protect our surviving freedoms?

Internationally, both the United Nations and the European Union have something to say. As early as 10 December 1948, the United Nations General Assembly adopted the Universal Declaration of Human Rights. Article 12 states:

> No one shall be subjected to arbitrary interference with his privacy, family, home or correspondence, nor to attacks upon his honour and reputation. Everyone has the right to the protection of the law against such interference or attacks.

Echoing such sentiments, the European Convention on Human Rights, article 8, states:

> Everyone has the right to respect for his private and family life, his home and his correspondence. There shall be no interference by a public authority with the exercise of this right except such as is in accordance with the law and is necessary in a democratic society in the interests of national security, public safety or the economic well-being of the country, for the prevention of disorder or crime, for the protection of health or morals, or for the protection of the rights and freedoms of others.

In 1976 the International Bill of Human Rights (which includes, *inter alia*, the Universal Declaration of Human Rights) took on the force of international law. The United Kingdom is therefore bound by the UN document and, in addition, the EU Convention has been incorporated into UK law. 'Freedom from arbitrary interference with privacy is therefore required by law and any interference with privacy must pass the test of necessity.'[1]

Unfortunately all these high-sounding declarations are honoured more in the breach than the observance. The problem is that these general instruments are (in common with most broad-stroke declarations that treat on basic rights and privileges) rarely specific enough to prevent wholesale abuse via innumerable semantic loopholes. In the context of the UN Declaration, what, for example, is meant by 'arbitrary'? Certainly, surveillance by private individuals may be effectively proscribed by this term; but if a government can circumvent this restriction merely by invoking 'national security', or a corporation by citing 'operational efficiency' – neither of which can be described as 'arbitrary interference' – then the proscription (and with it that part of the Declaration) is essentially meaningless.

In most cases it is left to legislatures at national or state level to delineate what is, and what is not, permissible within that jurisdiction. In most cases, such bodies have taken the easy way out and used an extremely narrow definition of privacy, with most of the legal restrictions framed in terms of safeguarding *individual* privacy, and more especially data protection. Precious little has been done with the aim of regulating surveillance, and this is an important omission given that surveillance has manifold deleterious effects other than simple invasion of individual privacy. Surveillance impacts on questions of human dignity, self-determination, social exclusion, basic justice and many others, which affect not merely individuals but whole groups and states (see next chapter). Such detrimental outcomes are not confined to tightly circumscribed parts of our life, but on the contrary now encompass most of the population's waking existence: our time at work, in public spaces, in shopping, at home, in our relations with the state, at borders, and when travelling. Ubicomp and AmI advances will undoubtedly add to the list and deepen disquiet.

Most privacy laws around the world are centred around ten 'Fair Information Principles' (FIPs) which require that organisations:

1. must be *accountable* for all the personal information in their possession;
2. should *identify the purposes* for which the information is processed at or before the time of collection;
3. should collect personal information only with the *knowledge and consent* of the individual (except under specified circumstances);
4. should *limit the collection* of personal information to that which is necessary for pursuing the identified purposes;
5. should not use or disclose personal information for purposes other than those identified, except with the consent of the individual (the finality principle);
6. should retain information only as long as necessary;
7. should ensure that personal information is kept accurate, complete and up-to-date;
8. should protect personal information with appropriate security safeguards;
9. should be open about their policies and practices and maintain no secret information system;
10. should allow data subjects access to their personal information, with an ability to amend it if it is inaccurate, incomplete or obsolete.[2]

We should be aware that these principles derive from the European Data Protection Directive 95/46/EC. As yet only data protection, and more specifically *individual* data protection, has been legislated for in any meaningful way. Even within this narrow field, the regulatory powers of the UK's foremost piece of 'privacy' legislation, the Data Protection Act 1998, leave much to be desired.

Despite the Act's size and reputation for complexity, and notwithstanding the provision of the Information Commissioner's

Office (ICO) to oversee its workings, the DPA remains a broken reed which does little to protect the public. Many of the key terms of the Act, even such basic concepts as 'personal information', are badly defined, making the provisions of the Act difficult to police. While the DPA does give citizens a small degree of control over their personal files, and may help curb governmental and business excesses in certain areas, it possesses serious limitations:

1. It is not really a privacy law, although the legislation is often portrayed as such in the media and by politicians themselves (the word 'privacy' is never mentioned anywhere in the Act). The DPA is an information law, dealing only with the way personal data are collected, stored, used and accessed. Surveillance and other related topics are not addressed.

2. There are the usual exemptions for national security, law enforcement and taxation, allowing the state to ride a coach and horses through any supposed protection.

3. It does nothing to prevent or limit the collection of information – a company can specify an almost unlimited number of functions and, provided the correct data protection form is completed and the fee paid, it is free to gather information 'relevant' to these functions.

4. The DPA does not prevent third parties getting access to our information without our permission.

5. The information commissioner is not provided with even the most rudimentary powers of a regulator – his investigative powers are limited and there is no provision for punitive penalties. The British Computer Society submitted that 'realistic penalties, including extraditable prison sentences, for the unauthorised

201

copying and provision or sale of personal information are seriously overdue'.[3] To its credit the ICO agrees, and has called for prison sentences of up to two years for such criminals.

6. There is no scope in the legislation to deal with international issues, making the law anachronistic in the global village of information export.

Both the DPA and ICO could, in fact, be counterproductive. Laws may be high-sounding, but if the regulator is ineffective and there are extensive exemptions for purposes of national security etc, are we really any better off? According to Privacy International, 'The existence of statutory privacy bodies, rather than impeding such trends, sometimes legitimates intrusive information practices'. The lack of 'joined-up government' within this sector, together with the redundancy between 'national regulatory bodies, confusion of responsibilities, and diverse interpretations of crucial concepts and terms', have hindered the logical allocation of roles between national and international regulatory bodies and impaired the implementation of even such weak legislation as presently exists.

Flawed though it undoubtedly is, the DPA is at least on the statute books. On surveillance and indeed freedom in general, UK law affords very little protection, and we are thrown back on human rights legislation which requires that everyone should have a 'reasonable expectation of privacy'. As with the 'arbitrary interference' phrase of the UN Declaration, 'a reasonable expectation of privacy' can mean different things to different people – we might, for example, confidently expect very different interpretations from a member of Liberty and an agent of MI5. 'Clarification of what counts as a reasonable expectation of privacy is necessary in order to protect this right and a public debate, including the legal, technical and political communities, should be encouraged in order to work towards a consensus on the definition of what is a "reasonable expectation".[4] Without such consensus, liberty in Britain will remain, as Geoffrey Robertson QC has said, 'a state of mind rather than a set of legal rules'.

The European Union seems to be travelling the same road. Although it has recently established the role of European Data Protection Supervisor (EDPS), it is, as its name suggests, once again focusing primarily on individual data protection, and not on the broader question of surveillance per se. The EDPS remit includes 'monitoring ICT [information and communication technology] and other developments, advising on and influencing European Community policies in regard to personal data processing, and the evolution of global and lower-level networks, meetings and discussions amongst privacy commissioners on important topics and technologies ...'[5] It is, in other words, a talking shop, with very little in the way of teeth to back up any recommendations it may make.

To make matters worse, traditional distinctions between privacy types are becoming blurred; with the increasing implementation of AmI and ubicomp systems, the old orthodox privacy arguments over 'privacy statements', 'opt-in/opt-out', 'choice', 'notice' etc are likely to become increasingly irrelevant as data flows seamlessly around an increasingly ubiquitous information net that monitors and caters for our every need. Nor should we forget the considerable number of 'computer illiterates' in our population, who will be effectively excluded from any discussions on the future direction of this 'new surveillance'.

The problems facing surveillance and privacy regulation, together with its Cinderella legal status, have led to a generally defeatist attitude in many quarters, and this has been encouraged by certain interests who wish to weaken public

203

and political support for regulatory measures. Scott McNealy, chief executive officer of Sun Microsystems, famously told a group of reporters and analysts: 'You have zero privacy anyway. Get over it.' Such propaganda is blatantly untrue (though certainly less so as time advances), but if repeated loudly and long enough may well become a self-fulfilling prophecy. Taken in conjunction with attempts to 'balance security and privacy' in a world kept in a state of constant fear, the advocates of privacy and surveillance regulation are unlikely to make much headway.

We should admit that there will *always* be an arm (or arms) of government who will act outside the law when it is expedient to do so. And it can be cogently argued that, under certain perilous conditions, such a facility is a prerequisite of state security and the personal well-being of its citizens. But in liberal democracies (as far as we know) such power to overshadow all aspects of a person's life has always been used *in extremis*, as a strategy of last resort against specific, clearly defined opponents. What we are seeing today is this final sanction deployed with apparent legality, on a routine basis, and against the entire civilian population. Why? Possibly because it can now be done easily and at very little cost, and bureaucrats take as much delight in accumulating data as a squirrel does in hoarding nuts. Or perhaps because every item of information secured tilts the balance of power more to the side of the political and industrial elite, whose main concern is to maintain the population as passive, acquiescent over-consumers of the goods which confer on these same elites both power and prestige. Whatever the motivation, it is this universal surveillance of our every move, purchase and aspiration that 'data protection' legislation has signally failed to hold in check.

Which raises a very pertinent question: even if dataveillance and similar technologies are legally justifiable, even if they help security and fight crime and tax evasion (and the case is far from proven), is their deployment wise socially? What are the ramifications for our society's cohesion and well-being?

13

CUMULATIVE IMPACT ON SOCIETY

Whatever reasons are advanced to defend the construction of the surveillance web, one thing is abundantly clear – the new technology is certain to change irrevocably the individual's place in society. More and more, technical means of control saturate modern existence, their tentacles reaching ever more sensitive areas of an individual's life, probing, sorting and documenting. Gary Marx, an MIT Professor Emeritus, has drawn our attention to the maximum security prison as an example of social surveillance and control in its most extreme form. With the increasing spread of surveillance throughout society, he asks, quite seriously, whether 'we are not moving toward becoming a maximum security society'. On present evidence, the answer must be a resounding 'Yes'.

One of the first casualties in a maximum security society is anonymity. Urban humanity has long cherished this aspect of privacy – an escape from the informal but nevertheless insistent surveillance of the village and other close-knit communities. Anonymity allows individuals to meet on relatively equal terms and to forge their own selfhood solely by their deeds and the relationships they maintain. Besides which, no one feels comfortable knowing that they are named and numbered and that their every action is being watched and logged. Unfortunately, with its emphasis on multiple ID systems, this is exactly what our population is being subjected to. When 'identity verification' is complete, in the form of a biometric ID card and a virtual, centralised National Identity Register, and the system rolled out on a nationwide and later a global scale, there will be, quite literally, nowhere to hide. Unlike in times past, the comforting idea of leaving your former mistakes behind, of upping sticks and beginning a new life in another part of the country (or, indeed, another part of the world) will be gone forever. Your identity and travel routes will be monitored with chilling efficiency – you will carry your triumphs, failures and lapses with you wherever you go ... there will be no second start in a new city or country for those whose personal identity is fused irrevocably to the 'surveillance superhighway'.

There is another danger here: that of uncritical enthusiasm for every new technological fix and the narrow belief that there is a specific IT answer to any particular problem. A system which may appear, theoretically, to offer the answer to one of society's ills (crime perhaps, or terrorism) often functions in an altogether different way in the complicated, messy arena of real life. It is ironic that many of the surveillance technologies that were initially invented to protect privacy (e.g. CCTV cameras in hotel corridors) now figure as invaders of our personal space.

The law of unintended consequences also casts its shadow over many crime prevention initiatives. CCTV surveillance of urban spaces was supposed to prevent crime; instead, as we've seen, the system merely transfers crime to different areas, and policing becomes reactive (watching for the crime to occur before taking action) rather than preventative. Again, RFID implants are touted as an answer to any number of identity scenarios, but end up implicated as facilitators of 'total surveillance' and instigators of cancer. The appearance of car-jacking is undoubtedly related to the development of better anti-theft devices in cars. When access keys prevent the simple stealing of cars, it does not necessarily follow that cars will not be stolen. Thieves may decide to confront the owner violently, beating or kidnapping the victim in order to obtain the required code, and what was a simple theft becomes something infinitely worse. Moreover, a narrow concentration on a 'technological fix' often has as its corollary the ignoring of wider issues or alternative methods. The technophile seeks a solution to every problem via technology and cannot see the wood for the trees; or again, in Gary Marx's telling phrase: 'To the person with a hammer, everything may look like a nail.'

Everyone a suspect

As we have seen in chapter 10, an important strand in the surveillance web – dataveillance – bids fair to stand many of our basic legal principles on their head. In times past, police and other bodies normally undertook investigation and monitoring after reasonable grounds for suspicion had arisen. Because mass dataveillance requires large numbers of subjects to be effective, the requirement of reasonable grounds has been abandoned; suspicion arises from the processing of thousands or millions of individuals, with a presumption of guilt shared by every member of the cohort under study. Dataveillance picks out suspects based on a number of assumptions written into the algorithm; if your profile ticks all the right boxes you will be automatically sorted into the suspect category. Proof of innocence is then required, rather than proof of guilt. This, in turn, will inevitably produce a fundamental change in the fabric of society. We will have to come to terms with the idea that we are all constantly under suspicion, that at any time, from a list of millions, the database may throw up our name as prime suspect and we will be required to demonstrate our innocence.

A question of trust

Just as worrying, heightened and sustained surveillance increases mistrust in any society, and places the always delicate social contract between individual and state under an intolerable pressure. Trust confers legitimacy in a democratic state and lack of trust in government of whatever political persuasion leads inevitably to poor performance at the ballot-box. This is not to say that disapproval of governments who implement intrusive surveillance systems will stop such practices; it was not the present administration who proposed ID cards, but an unelected bureaucracy (see page 30). At most, electorate disenchantment with some surveillance technologies may slow down their deployment but, as we've seen with ID cards and e-passports (and, one might add, a European Constitution masquerading as a treaty), with some projects the people's disapproval counts for very little – they are rolled out regardless. Then again, once sufficient surveillance systems are in place and resistance difficult, if not impossible, why should those controlling the surveillance net take cognisance of any protestor?

No less a figure than Sir John Smith, former deputy commissioner of the Metropolitan Police, has voiced his concerns over the question of trust. As early as 1995 (long before worries concerning RFID chips or ID cards had surfaced), he claimed that the UK was becoming an Orwellian society. Modern surveillance systems implemented since that time (for example, the huge increase in CCTV, rampant dataveillance and RFID ID cards, along with the National Identity Register) can only exacerbate this deepening divide between citizen and state. The effect will likely be most marked in ethnic minority communities, who are already subject to more frequent 'stop and search' than the majority white population. Baroness Helena Kennedy QC, in considering the effect of ID cards in other countries, notes that French lawyers 'are clear that *les marginaux* are harassed to produce the [French ID] card and it affects the culture of policing negatively'.[1] Sir John Smith argued that the growth of surveillance would inevitably provoke distrust and distance the citizen from the state. What price then 'policing by consent'?

Choice and consent

Consent implies a choice: that we can say either yes or no to any particular option on offer. And choice is a favourite buzz-word of New Labour spokesmen; we have, we are told, choice in education, consumer choice of products, patient choice of hospital. In the latter case, once we have chosen our hospital, we are asked to consent to a particular treatment, or to agree that our personal medical information be transferred or used in a research programme. In each situation, the facts and possible consequences are carefully explained so that the patient may make what has come to be called 'informed patient consent'. This is well and good; medical records are a form of surveillance and it is right that the individual concerned can refuse any procedure they may find offensive.

Unfortunately, outside of medicine, the citizen has few powers of veto over other forms of surveillance. Anyone wishing to function in modern society must simply accept the fact that, willy nilly, they will be watched in numerous ways. Are we seriously expected to believe that we can refuse to be surveilled? Do we consent to numerous CCTV cameras following and recording our movements though urban centres? And which

211

motorists have ever consented to having their vehicle movements logged at the ACPO's ANPR centre? 'Arrestees do not consent, and are coerced, into providing fingerprint and DNA samples, which will be permanently logged on the police national database, even if they are released without charge.' 'Informed consent' is likewise impossible: 'It is almost impossible for a person to know how information is being used, and how it may, in subtle ways, affect their lives; for instance, by increasing the chances that their vehicle is stopped by the police, or the demand that they pay in advance for goods and services.'[2]

Social exclusion and speed of access

Oscar Gandy coined the term 'panoptic sort' to describe the systematic categorisation of a population to a hitherto unimagined degree. Alan Wexelblat of the MIT Media Lab's Software Agents Group has described the purpose of the panoptic sort as being 'to enable information-holders to make predictions about the behavior of the people on whom the information was collected. The ultimate goal is to be able to sort all the people the company comes in contact with along whatever dimension of information is desired.' The panoptic sort is datamining writ large.

Combined with a national numbering system which identifies and combines each sub-persona of our public personality (employee, supermarket consumer, homeowner, vehicle owner and the rest), such social sorting operations will inevitably lead to discrimination, social exclusion and a lessening of societal cohesion.

Exclusion can be as simple as selling goods at different prices to different people, as has happened already with Amazon.com's fluctuating selling-price for DVDs according to an individual's position in that company's sorting system, based on previous purchasing history. Such practices can only increase as auto-mated RFID surveillance in products and clothes become commonplace.

In our increasingly congested and high-speed society, those with wealth and education tend to possess identification systems (be it a frequent flyer card or a credit card) which expedite movement and purchasing. Those without such cards, or those whose card details carry a negative value, increasingly find their passage through various systems impeded. It is well known that answering services at most banks operate a tiered response: while 'low value' clients languish on hold, those customers deemed valuable to the bank receive immediate attention. A further problem is that much of this social sorting uses soft-ware that works 24/7, with an instantaneous response that lacks the mediating, discretionary skills of a human opera-tive.[3] CCTV systems operate under the same disadvantage; increasingly algorithms decide what is, and what is not, a suspicious behaviour/appearance/identifier. So what criteria and discriminatory biases have been introduced when the code is written? As Ericson and Shearing have demonstrated, there is an aura of legitimacy surrounding both law and science which constrains critical questioning.[4] Because technological controls such as CCTV epitomise both law and science, we tend to assume that they must be valid, objective and fair. We must learn to question these assumptions and to understand that the benefits claimed are socially interpreted, and that both political and commercial agents may have a vested interest in 'talking up' the technology while at the same time suppressing its negative social impact.

The continued collection of more and more data categories can only lead to increased social sorting, with all the implica-tions that has for the development of a two-tier society containing first- and second-class citizens, 'threatening a technological lock-in dividing contemporary societies more decisively into high-speed, high-mobility and connected and low-speed, low-mobility and disconnected classes.'[5]

When things go wrong

Such concerns demand debate and public awareness of the problem. But note that all these problems tacitly assume the efficient working of the surveillance web; that ID cards, facial recognition, phone intercepts, massive data-matching abilities, and the rest of the paraphernalia of surveillance will all function faultlessly. This is far from being the case.

On 2 August 2002, the sum of $300,000 in damages was awarded by a court in Portland, Oregon to Roger Benson, who had been wrongfully imprisoned for 43 days. Benson's nightmare began in California on 6 February 1998, when he was pulled over for a motoring offence and fingerprinted. The system used by the California police, Livescan, produced an Electronic Fingerprint Card (EFC) and a unique identifier, the fingerprint control number (FPN).

But the process malfunctioned, and in September 1998 another man, William Lee Kellogg, was charged with multiple felonies and entered on the system with the same FPN as Benson. The duplicate records were added to the Oregon Judicial Information Network (OJIN), where Kellogg's criminal record was attached to Benson's file. As far as the database was concerned, Benson was a three-times-convicted felon. The following year, when the California police pulled Benson over and found a (perfectly legal) handgun in his truck, the computer told the lawmen he was in breach of the California Penal Code and, despite protesting his innocence, he was thrown into prison.[6]

This incident is not unique. Miguel and Lilia Espinoza ran a busy restaurant in Medford, Oregon until a local newspaper falsely reported that he had been convicted of homicide and sent to prison. Once again, an incorrect criminal record had been attached to an innocent man. 'People just stopped coming to the restaurant,' said Mrs Espinoza. 'Some people came in to tell me they were sorry my husband was in prison, but nobody came by to order food. Business just died.'

The Espinozas sued in a class action filed in July 2004. Their lawyer, Charles Carreon, is forthright about the problem. 'The OSP (Oregon State Police) has known about the problem in their criminal history database since 1998 [i.e., since the Benson incident], but they are concealing the problem to avoid liability, even as more innocent people fall victims to a nightmare scenario.' The source of the problem, says Carreon, starts with 'the Livescan machine giving two people the same fingerprint control number, and ends with the State of Oregon creating false criminal histories that are forwarded to the FBI and all fifty states.' As a result, 'one person, like Mr Benson or Mr Espinoza, is reported to local police as a felon, resulting in identity-theft by the State!'[7]

The system used in both these farragoes of justice, Livescan, was made by the American company Identix (slogan: 'Empowering Identification'). In 2004, the company won a US Department of Homeland Security Blanket Purchase Agreement (BPA) for fingerprint systems. Identix is also supplying equipment for the UK Identity and Passport Service's ID card trial. The potential for an epidemic of false convictions, by a system that has already put innocent people in jail, is very real indeed.

The problem lies in the old 'rubbish in rubbish out' predicament that has dogged computers ever since their inception. While police, NHS and other databases seem to sprout into being overnight, like so many silicon mushrooms, the truth is that

215

every bit, byte and kilobyte of information has at one time or another been inputted by a human or via software written by our species. The data to be uploaded must also be collected and stored. And each of these stages (gathering of samples, recording, labelling and input) is subject to the same fallibilities, falsities and corruption as any other area of human endeavour. According to British Columbia's *Times Colonist* (10 October 2006), more than a dozen people in BC have been wrongfully arrested in recent years because of clerical errors by court staff. 'The records, obtained through the Freedom of Information Act, reveal that people have spent as long as 17 days behind bars simply because a court clerk typed "remand" into the court computer instead of a "release".' Compounding this, the transfer of false information between computer databases means that the further the error spreads, the harder it becomes to correct the file. And the higher the confidence in the system, the lower the chances of obtaining a fair hearing. We have all experienced problems when a computer fails, as when one's bank wrongly rejects one's credit card. Complaining at such times is often an exercise in futility – it is invariably 'the computer' that is believed.

Such cares pale in comparison to the havoc that a failure of the surveillance web would produce for an unlucky individual. Problems skyrocket with increasing complexity: computer error compounds exponentially within a labyrinthine and multi-level system. And when they fail it is inevitably the 'customer' who suffers. We see regular stories of credit reference agencies misidentifying individuals who, as a result of the information web already in place, find it impossible to obtain loans or hire-purchase agreements from any supplier until they have formally proven that the information held on them is false. How much more disastrous might this be in the brave new world of ID cards, when every aspect of our existence is held and cross-referenced – lives and reputations may be ruined by a misplaced keystroke.

Or a misplaced CD. The loss (made public on 20 November 2007 after nearly six weeks' delay) of the personal data of 25 million individuals is not simply an example of rank government incompetence – it is a wake-up call for the disasters that await every man, woman or child who has been persuaded to give up detailed information for inclusion in the burgeoning list of mega-databases set up by corporate and governmental bureaucrats. Despite having in place what appear to have been reasonable security procedures, a decision to ignore these same procedures resulted in the names, addresses, national insurance numbers and bank details of 7.5 million families being granted no more security than an ordinary letter – sent from Washington, Tyne and Wear to the National Audit Office in London like a normal piece of mail: dropped in the post room for collection by a courier. And when the package failed to arrive, an identical pair of CDs, unencrypted like the first, was sent off, this time by registered post. It would be impossible to make this up.

Should the lost data find its way into criminal hands, the fraudsters have all they need to obtain credit cards and mobile phone contracts, or to open a false bank account and go on a spending spree. And although assurances were given that there was not enough information on the disks to access bank accounts directly, the truth is somewhat different. Adults often use one of their children's names as a bank password, and – as these same children's names are included in the missing data – a sizeable percentage of the 7.5 million accounts must be deemed at risk. Failing that, technology can be bought over the net that allows a fraudster to try millions of possible passwords in minutes. The potential for chaos is enormous.

But it could have been much, much worse. Imagine a similar

scenario, just a year or two hence, in which the data of 25 million individuals held by the Identity and Passport Service, or on the National Identity Register, was compromised. Criminals and ID thieves would then possess biometric data on each individual. No possibility here of closing bank accounts, or demanding the government bring in new national insurance numbers; as we've seen, biometric data is unchangeable, lifelong. There would be no way, short of dying, of making the lost data invalid. And yet the UK government's response is to press on with biometric collection, and even to claim that ID cards would have helped prevent this farrago. Such an attitude can only lead to further catastrophe.

The much vaunted DNA database is an excellent case in point. While the government pushes for greater and greater inclusion of individuals' DNA, it is careful to avoid mention of the fact that the chances of a mismatch *increase* as the database grows. DNA matching is probabilistic rather than positive, as Professor Peter Taylor Gooby and many other academics have pointed out. In essence, when comparing small numbers of individuals to a suspect sample, the chances of compelling similarity are extremely remote; but become less so as the subject number rises. Imagine an island with 50 inhabitants and a murder victim who, with his dying breath, whispered 'Quentin killed me'. Chances are, there will be only one Quentin among the 50 islanders, so identification can be pretty well conclusive. But in a city like London, with a population of 7 million, there will be many, many more 'Quentins', and a far greater chance of wrongful arrest and conviction. The same is true of the national DNA database: the more people listed, the higher the probability that you or I may find ourselves in police custody for a crime we did not commit, based solely on the structure of the base pairs in our DNA. Scientific fallibility aside, the possibility of wrongful conviction from planted evidence and other abuses is a not wholly irrational fear.

Non-inclusion on the national DNA database does not guarantee freedom from scrutiny. Section 60 of the Health and Social Care Act 2001 quietly introduced the right of the Secretary of State to allow the accessing of medical records if, in his opinion, it is in the public interest to do so. 'This means that the procedures are already in place to allow police investigating crime to apply to a politician so that computerised medical records can be trawled.'[8] And not only DNA.

Given the weight that is attached to DNA evidence, we should be very concerned about security arrangements governing any storage of, and access to, such information. There have already been several cases of policemen selling data and information to criminals and the press. DNA data is far more valuable and could command much higher prices than, say, the home address of a celebrity or a politician's sexual peccadilloes. Insurance companies and criminals alike may be willing to pay to access this information.

Of course, government scoffs at any idea of a Big Brother aspect to DNA collection. But spin aside, a good indication of their true feelings on the matter became apparent when a former Attorney General, the late Lord Williams, stated his theoretical willingness to give a DNA sample if, say, a child in his village were the victim of crime. Baroness Helena Kennedy followed up on the noble peer's musings and asked whether all Cabinet ministers would set an example to the general populace by putting their own DNA on the database. Tellingly, there was no substantive response to this reasonable request, and not a single minister subsequently rose to the challenge. Baroness Kennedy also comments: 'It is worth noting that the police themselves have shown a marked reluctance to be included for elimination purposes, in case the information might be used in paternity suits, or by the Child Support Agency or in disciplinary proceedings.' When both politicians and police show a marked lack of personal commitment to an enterprise they espouse so enthusiastically in public, we have every right to be suspicious – and to do whatever lies within our power to resist.

14

WATCHING THE WATCHERS –
WHAT WE CAN DO TO RESIST

Knowledge of the depth and extent of the potential dangers facing our society often leaves people feeling understandably dazed and powerless. But the story is not one of unremitting gloom.

Sousveillance and public opinion

To some degree, surveillance cuts both ways. Thanks to the prevalence of video and phone cameras, ordinary citizens now have a means of 'watching the watchers' and recording their observations, an activity known as 'sousveillance' (literally 'watching from below'). Although many 'sousveillance events' are little more than self-indulgent stunts (World Sousveillance Day appears to have involved nothing more provocative than taking still photographs of CCTV cameras), other activists have had major impacts on society. Sousveillance does offer the possibility of logging at least some of the corrupt or illegal practices of the authorities and their agents in such detail that there is no opportunity for 'plausible deniability'.

Perhaps the first effective example of watching the watcher occurred on 3 March 1991 when George Holliday filmed four officers of the LAPD mercilessly beating a lone black man,

Rodney King. King was on parole for a robbery conviction at the time, had failed to stop the car he was driving and had jumped several red lights and stop signs before he was pulled over. The police claimed that King had tried to resist arrest and continued to resist even while being hit with batons. However, the video showed King immobile on the ground and the police continuing to belabour his inert body regardless. The incident became something of a *cause célèbre* and was a major factor in the LA riots a year later. During the ensuing trial only one of the policemen was found guilty, partly because a segment of the video (not widely shown by the media) showed King getting up and attacking a policeman.

More recently, in November 2006, widely-viewed footage on YouTube revealed a UCLA police officer assaulting a student in the university library. The important point here is not merely the act of sousveillance, but the publicising of examples of abuse to the widest possible audience. For example, in August 2007 three police officers of the Sûreté du Québec (Quebec Police) infiltrated a demonstration against the leaders of Canada, Mexico and the United States at a meeting of the Security and Prosperity Partnership (SPP) in Montebello, Quebec. The demonstrators claimed that the officers were *agents provocateurs*, there to provoke an incident that would discredit the demonstration and allow the deployment of riot police. When the head of the Quebec police denied the allegations and publicly stated that there had been no police presence, a sousveillance video screened on YouTube revealed that he was lying. He quickly revised his statement to say that while police might have been placed among the protestors, they were there as peaceful observers only. Scrutiny of the sousveillance video showed them to be masked, wearing police boots, with at least one holding a rock. At one point Dave Coles, president of the Communications, Energy and Paperworkers Union, had to order the three masked police 'observers' away from a confrontation with the line of riot police.

The practice of sousveillance has now spread to the developing world. Organisations such as 'Witness' in the USA lend video equipment to human rights activists around the globe, and have led to exposés such as Operation Fine Girl, detailing rape as a weapon of war in Sierra Leone.[1]

But despite such advantages, the balance of power remains vastly in favour of the Big Boys, whose technological reach and firepower will always vastly outweigh that of the individual or action group. Regulation in the form of 'codes of practice' is regularly ignored; legal restrictions are flouted, or made obsolete by rapidly changing technology. Those attempting to implement the global surveillance strategy can only be defeated by a groundswell of public opinion, and by privacy activists willing to fight a long, sustained campaign to raise public awareness. There are parallels here to the eco-warriors of the 70s – dismissed for decades as 'idealistic greenies', they refused to buy into the 'resistance is futile' or 'this is progress' mantras that are promoted so consistently and so effectively by both government and major corporations. Many commentators felt that their goals, though laudable, were idealistic and unrealistic. Yet the eco-warriors persisted, and today much of their agenda is now accepted as mainstream.

Australia provides a perfect, and timely, example of the need for public awareness and the power of public opinion. In 1986 the Australian government signalled its intention of issuing a national identity card (the Australia Card Bill, or ACB). The rationale behind the move was the usual mix of catching benefit frauds and apprehending illegal immigrants, with the added implication that 'only those with something to hide had something to fear'. Most Australians were quickly sold on the idea, with opinion polls showing an 80 per cent approval of the proposal.

Then, slowly at first, but with increasing insistence, questions began to be asked on civil liberties and privacy. When the public heard that the number of government departments intending to require the ID card had leaped from three to 30 their suspicions grew, and were confirmed by the minutiae of the Bill, which listed a host of restrictive penalties. Cardless persons could not be hired or paid (fine for doing so: A$20,000), would be denied access to pre-existing bank accounts, could not cash in investments, give or receive money from a solicitor, or receive funds from unit trusts. They could not buy or rent their own home. If your card was destroyed and you could not prove that its loss was accidental there was a $5,000 fine or two years in prison (or both). Failure to produce your ID on demand at a tax office incurred a A$20,000 penalty. Cardless sick and unemployed people, pensioners, widows and invalids would be denied benefits.

Nor was this likely to be the limit of the repressive measures envisioned for the people of Australia. Aware of possible resistance, the card's architect, the Health Insurance Commission, suggested a plan which discussed the incremental stealth strategy used in so many surveillance proposals with surprising honesty:

> One possibility would be to use a staged approach for implementation, whereby only less sensitive data are held in the system initially, with the facility to input additional data at a later stage when public acceptance may be forthcoming more readily.

A parliamentary joint select committee found against the card, pointing out the serious civil liberties implications and warning of a fundamental change in the relationship between citizen and state. Newspapers on the right and left raised their voice against the Bill and many famous Australians joined the clamour. Public opinion, now fully informed, swung solidly against the

ID card and within a few weeks the 80 per cent approval had metamorphosed into an astonishing 90 per cent opposition to the Bill. Faced with a protest of monumental proportions, the government backed down.

It would be nice to report that the victory was permanent. Unfortunately, Thomas Jefferson's old adage on freedom[2] applies with a vengeance to surveillance. While the Australian public quickly lost interest in the ID card issue, their rulers simply bided their time. Two decades later the concept reappeared, when former Australian Prime Minister John Howard announced a scheme (national card; linked to a massive central database; essential to stop fraud and benefit cheats etc) that looked suspiciously like the old ID card idea. But Mr Howard insisted that the two concepts were poles apart and engaged in some outrageous doublespeak to prove it. Just as the UK ID card had become an Entitlement Card, so now the Australian ID was metamorphosed by the magic of political sophistry into the all-new Access Card. Nor was the card to be mandatory for all Australians. 'It will not be compulsory to have the card,' Howard told journalists, adding however that 'it will be necessary for everybody who needs a card to apply for one.' As, from 2010, the provision of health and social services will be denied anyone without an Access Card, then except for those guaranteed lifelong health and prosperity, the card is essential to all Australians. Surprisingly, the scam seems to have worked; the lessons of the 80s have been lost, and a step-wise, stealthy approach has lulled a continent's population into acceptance. This is all the more surprising when other, less intrusive methods of establishing identity are now available.

Designing out surveillance: the privacy card

The UK administration, along with many Western governments, continues to insist on the necessity of ID cards linked to massive databases. These databases, and their interconnectivity, are responsible for a huge number of privacy and civil liberty concerns, not least of which is dataveillance. But as much as the UK government might wish it, there is simply no need for biometric patterns on ID cards, e-passports and the like to be checked against a central database. The pattern can be stored within the smart card itself, with the comparison exercise being performed within the card – which would then say simply 'Yes' or 'No' to the system. In the case of e-passports with finger-print biometrics, the owner of the passport would place their digit against a fingerprint reader which would then capture the data and convert it to a transitory biometric template. The machine would then electronically interrogate the e-passport and determine if the pattern it had just recorded was the same as the pattern held on the passport. If the patterns matched, identity would be confirmed – and all without resort to any central database.

We can have secure identity without recourse to centralisation. Indeed, there are no technological barriers to the production of a comprehensive 'privacy card' which would act as a buffer to prevent information being centralised. Such a card could disguise the identity of its owner and scramble personal information so as to prevent the collection of sensitive data in large databases by large organisations.

Of course, such cards would still depend upon RFID technology to be effective, leaving the owner vulnerable to a scanning attack by illicit card readers, and a consequent risk of ID theft if the encryption protecting the data is broken (not to mention the location and surveillance dangers of the technology). Unless we forgo RFID entirely there does not seem to be any way of avoiding such threats. But rejecting RFID passports is by no means a bad idea – other more secure methods of checking and verifying such documents already exist.

Ingenia Technology have developed 'Laser Surface Authentication' (LSA) which allows any document, including a passport or ID card, to be positively identified by virtue of its unique individual surface qualities.[3] When paper or plastic laminate is made, each sheet 'sets' in a one-off configuration dependent on a variety of factors such as fibre orientation, temperature and humidity. The surface of each sheet is as unique as a human fingerprint – it is impossible to counterfeit. The newly-developed Ingenia technology can scan any document to reveal this 'LSA fingerprint' of its surface properties. The system dispenses with any data chip; it is 'read-only' and, once scanned, a record of the document's surface features is stored on a database along with non-biometric details of its owner. When the document is rescanned the appropriate details – name, address, etc, of the owner – can be instantly displayed.

This is a highly accurate system, which not only makes false matching unlikely but allows counterfeit passports to be detected immediately (those documents lacking a database presence would be invalid), and can even detect whether a photograph or name has been altered.

The Royal Academy of Engineering has pointed out that LSA scanning is far more secure than the government-favoured RFID solution. In addition, the Academy's report points out that it 'could also offer privacy gains, as the amount of information on the database available to the person scanning a passport can be controlled – it could be limited to just a name or a photo or even just the assurance that the passport is a genuine passport issued by the appropriate country. This technology could be used for ID cards. Instead of ID cards having chips on them or information printed on their surface, they could be linked to databases in the same way. Provided the database is secure, then individuals' privacy and security is protected. Alternatively, more advanced privacy schemes are possible where the LSA fingerprint is used as an encryption key for locally held personal information. Traditional technologies such as 2D barcodes can be used to carry the information on the card itself. This offers the same immutability of data as would occur if it was held on a central database, combined with the inability to make identical copies.'[4]

Instead of using such advances that could easily circumvent the known vulnerabilities of RFID-based cards, the UK government (and now the European Union) seems hell-bent on deploying one of the few systems *which absolutely require* the establishment of huge central databases. The question is, of course, why? And the next, *cui bono*? It is most definitely not the citizen. Bureaucracy and big business are the only winners here.

LSA scanning is just one of a number of privacy-enhancing technologies (PETs) which essentially act as countermeasures against the PITs (privacy invasive technologies). The web can be surfed anonymously via sites such as Turbohide.com; web 'cookies' can be filtered; encryption of personal data can prevent corporations (though not governments) from obtaining data; network design and software code can produce a marked regulatory effect;[5] privacy preference tools and smart agents can likewise help to keep the surveillance society at bay. But most countermeasures are for the computer aficionado – those lacking knowledge, awareness or even the wherewithal to implement the available PETs will always remain in the majority.

Some forms of electronic communication, such as email, are still possible anonymously via 'remailers' and other arrangements, who manage a succession of intermediary-operated services in which (like cells in a resistance or espionage organisation) each intermediary knows only the identity of those adjacent to it in the chain. 'Pseudonymity' is also possible, where substantial protections are put in place, but can be removed under defined legal circumstances. While 'anonymity' sites raise questions of what purpose they may ultimately serve (criminal and terrorist organisations will find them particularly useful), 'pseudonymity' has its own problems, in that the power to override protections is normally in the hands of government or corporations and, as Roger Clarke has commented, 'governments throughout history have shown themselves to be untrustworthy when their interests are too seriously threatened; and corporations are dedicated to shareholder value alone ...'[6]

Privacy Impact Assessment

The similarities between the environmental protests of the 1970s and today's anti-surveillance activism point up a method to slow down or stop the deployment of harmful surveillance systems. With our 'greener' perceptions, the Environmental Impact Assessment (EIA) is now accepted practice throughout the developed world whenever new building or infrastructure developments are mooted. An EIA allows for a review, in advance of any building work, of any possible environmental effects that may accrue from the proposed project. Recently, there have been demands that a similar Privacy Impact Assessment (PIA) be required before the rollout of new surveillance procedures. This call has been heeded in some countries, and both the USA and Canada have mandated the technique for all federal-level, public-sector projects where personal data is processed. So far the UK government has shown interest in the idea, but without moving to any mandatory requirement. This is unfortunate, as at present new information systems and methods of processing and transferring data between and across departments are often established with little or no regard for privacy concerns. When things go wrong, operators are faced with the challenge of mending the system, often with costly 'bolt-on' solutions that compromise efficiency. Or, as often as not, the problem is simply ignored. A report for the information commissioner by the Surveillance Studies Network explained that, in simple terms, a PIA may be seen as:

- 'an assessment of any actual or potential effects that an activity or proposal may have on individual privacy and the ways in which any adverse effects may be mitigated.'[7]

- 'a process. The fact of going through this process and examining the options will bring forth a host of alternatives which may not otherwise have been considered.'[8]

- an approach and a philosophy that holds promise by instilling a more effective culture of understanding and practice within organisations that process personal data.

- a form of risk assessment, which therefore cannot escape the uncertainties of identifying and estimating the severity and likelihood of the various risks that may appear to privacy, life chances, discrimination, equality and so on.

- a tool for opening up the proposed technologies or applications to in-depth scrutiny, debate and precautionary action within the organisation(s) involved.

- like PETs, premised on the view that it is better to build safeguards in than to bolt them on.

- an early-warning technique for decision-makers and operators of systems that process personal information, enabling them to understand and resolve conflicts between their aims and practices, and the required protection of privacy as set out above or the control of surveillance.

- Ideally, a public document leading to gains in transparency and in the elevation of public awareness of surveillance issues and dangers may be realised; in turn, it may assist regulatory bodies in carrying out their work effectively.

PIAs are long overdue in the United Kingdom, but they are not the whole story. As we have seen, surveillance encompasses more than simple privacy concerns. The time is ripe for an expansion of the PIA concept to one of Surveillance Impact Assessment (SIA), allowing for a review which would encompass the totality of surveillance effects, both individual and societal.[9] As the Surveillance Studies Network report states:

> What an ICT innovation, a new database, or a new audio-visual scheme for monitoring public places or private shopping precincts implies for personal autonomy and dignity, social solidarity, or the texture of social interactions, is not an inconceivable line of enquiry that could become institutionalised as a set of practices and requirements before those surveillance possibilities are implemented.[10]

Despite it being merely common sense and natural justice to ask such basic questions, such a Surveillance Impact Assessment requirement would demand a painful shift of worldview for government, corporations, and privacy regulators alike. But it is a change they must make if we are to support and maintain such basic values as trust, goodwill and a belief in the democratic process within our increasingly fractured society.

Direct action

If all else fails, it is still possible to organise effective protests against some of the worst excesses of the surveillance society. It is surprising how much surveillance actually depends upon the cooperation or acquiescence of the individual under observation or from whom data is required. The UK government's own figures – made public grudgingly, after three years' delay – reveal that 30 per cent of the UK population is predicted to refuse to cooperate with ID card checks. Should this figure rise to over 50 per cent (as may well occur when the full impact of the ID legislation becomes apparent), the whole scheme could well become unworkable. In addition, workers in the surveillance business may have philosophical issues about the use to which the data they collect is put; they can quite easily disrupt or modify this data collection, degrading its value.

Using cash and postal mail services serves to disconnect you, to some degree, from the surveillance web. Refusing store cards of any colour prevents further entries under your name on marketing lists; obtaining cards in false names further confuses the marketers (anti-surveillance advocate and former MIT professor Gary Marx has obtained store cards in the names of both Karl and Groucho Marx). In a similar way, forms and documents that demand an overabundance of personal details may be filled out with imaginary information. Small errors in the spelling of names, addresses and other details will create multiple entries in the databases and make successful data-matching less likely. Workers who key in information from forms can similarly introduce deliberate mistakes, and even greater disruption is possible from computer programmers erasing data-bases (and backups), or introducing logic bombs, Trojan horses and similar disruptive programmes. As Brian Martin has pointed out, a simple magnet can corrupt computer disks. It is even possible to make your own RFID 'fryer' to frustrate clothing tags and ID cards alike, although this practice is fraught with risk and should be discouraged.

Unfortunately, such methods have serious limitations: they may have nuisance value but, given the size and complexity of the surveillance web, they are little more than pinpricks in the hide of the surveillance behemoth. And they are *individual* acts, performed for the most part in secrecy. But other, more overt strategies are possible.

The south coast town of Brighton is not normally associated with direct action in any shape or form. But on 10 May 1997, two hundred individuals joined together in what was Britain's first coordinated attack on a CCTV camera system. According to one activist magazine, 'Public ridicule of surveillance cameras is effective in diminishing their power – and more importantly their dignity – and making them highly visible to people who have simply got used [to them] as street furniture.'[11] The protestors were creative in their approach: over 2,000 black and yellow posters carrying the words 'WARNING You Are Being Watched By Closed Circuit Television' were stuck up in toilets and other public spaces, provoking argument and indignation; lasers were used to 'blind' the cameras; posts carrying the cameras were 'occupied'; one camera was hoodwinked with a bag; the high-light of the day came 'when a blow-up doll, the sort available from sex shops, was hoisted to the top of a camera pole and

233

some rather embarrassed firefighters were dispatched with their ladders to remove her'.[12]

The protestors demonstrated a sophisticated knowledge of both the psychology and the technology of CCTV:

More fun can be had trying to destabilise the confidence in the relationship between the camera operator and the police on the ground. For example, some sea-front boy racers were caught pouring liquid from a petrol can onto a car in front of a CCTV camera. When the police raced to the scene, the lads got out some sponges and said they were just cleaning it (the can contained water) ... Making plays in front of a range of cameras simultaneously sends a direct message to the control room that we are watching them watching us. Identical masks can be used for protection and confusion ... Many cameras use microwaves to send information back to the central control room, and these can be disabled using reflective industrial foil strips attached to helium-filled balloons at the correct height. Camera poles can be useful 'Lost Children Stations'. Simply make a sign and give balloons to children waiting under the cameras. Now who would take a balloon off a child?

But despite the satisfaction such demonstrations engender, we should not fool ourselves. Present resistance efforts are better than nothing, but they still take place within a general and growing surveillance environment – small victories do not equate to a dismantling of the panoptic whole. 'Who will watch the watchers?' is a critical question; but then, so is 'Who will watch the watchers of the watchers?' and so on *ad nauseam*. The truth is that even with the biggest budgets, the most advanced technology and the best will in the world, no system we can set in place will be invulnerable to subversion. Human ingenuity combined with human craving for superiority and power will always find a way around restrictions. Examples abound: the Constitution of the United States of America explicitly states that control of the nation's money supply should rest with the state. And yet we have a private bank (the cunningly named Federal Reserve, which has nothing to do with the US government and can be found, should you choose to look, among the white 'business pages' of the US telephone directory), co-owned by seven private banks, at least three of whom are not even US entities, doing just that and essentially dictating the economy of the USA. Despite appearances to the contrary, Alan Greenspan and his successors are private businessmen to a man.

That such a subterfuge can be perpetrated on the American people, against the explicit prohibition of the Constitution, is a timely 'heads-up' to all those concerned with the intrusive nature of modern corporate and governmental structures; we must beware of taking appearance for substance, of confusing high-sounding declarations, voluntary codes and toothless legislation for effective regulation and relevant laws that will vigorously pursue any miscreant with custodial deterrent sentences. The surveillance network is huge, and continues to expand and pry into ever more sensitive areas of our lives. Only comprehensive legislation, and the outright banning of some of its more intrusive offshoots, will control surveillance's worst excesses. Individuals and pressure groups can help cut holes in the surveillance web, but until public opinion sets its weight behind such lone voices, it will be difficult indeed to stem the tide. As Ericson and Haggerty have pointed out: 'In the face of multiple connections across myriad technologies and practices, struggles against particular manifestations of surveillance, as important as they might be, are akin to efforts to keep the ocean's tide back with a broom – a frantic focus on a particular unpalatable technology or practice while the general tide of surveillance washes over us all.'[13]

EPILOGUE

There is little doubt that there are benefits from the implementation of most of the surveillance technologies. Financial benefits include the potential prevention of some tax and social welfare fraud for government, and financial and insurance scams in the private sector. The physical security of both people and property may be enhanced by their use, at least as regards certain petty small-scale crimes. However, it would be a mistake to believe that we have here a simple, obvious trade-off between security and privacy. Acceptance of New Labour's much-trailed identity card (aka Entitlement Card) is often promoted as a take-it-or-leave-it choice between carrying this data-dense document and further terrorist bombing. And this despite the fact that, on 3 July 2004, the then home secretary David Blunkett stated: 'I accept that it is important that we do not pretend that an entitlement card would be an overwhelming factor in combating international terrorism.' Also in 2004, Privacy International published the only research then conducted on ID cards and terrorism: it found that almost two-thirds of known terrorists operate under their real identity, and concluded that 'the presence of an ID card is not recognised by analysts as a meaningful or significant component in anti-terrorism strategies'. As in so many other instances, the amount of information sought by governments is far in excess of the potential security advantages that can be obtained. Nor is it clear that the enormous sums spent on such technology might not produce better results were the funds to be directed elsewhere.

There can be few objections to the use of IT and limited dataveillance within a given organisation, to aid its general productivity. Indeed, companies averse to using such tools are likely to languish behind their competitors. However, cogent arguments can be advanced against the depth and extent of such scrutiny, which often exceeds the requirements of the stated problem. This is especially true when government dataveillance is considered, and the system takes on a sinister cast when such limited databases are collated in the form of 'LifeLogs'.

Although this book is intended primarily as an overview of the surveillance technologies to which we are all subjected, and the possible outcomes of their implementation, surveillance itself is merely a part of an even bigger picture of control by stealth. We should not lose sight of the fact that our legal freedoms and rights have been gradually eroded over the past several decades, that Big Pharma has obtained an ever-increasing hold on medical practice, that agribusiness has done its utmost to destroy traditional (organic) farming practices, that science is increasingly financed by corporations with their own vested interests, that political parties (especially in the 'power house of democracy', the USA) are utterly reliant on the donations of major corporations, and that reporting of these and many more abuses is inadequately covered, and often ignored, by a supine and acquiescent mass media (much of which is owned, or heavily influenced via advertising and other pathways, by Big Business).

This is not simply a concern with the gradual establishment of totalitarian governments within democratic nations, though this danger is real enough. Mass surveillance is clearly an arbitrary action. In a democratic state, with rare exceptions such as national emergencies, police forces are not granted the power to interfere with citizens without due cause. The procedures of dataveillance turn such safeguards on their head, because no suspicion exists prior to the investigation. Thus, even without a totally repressive regime, individual liberties may be significantly compromised.

Compounding this, there is a danger that individuals may be incorrectly identified, which, given the desire to collate and form national databases, may lead to extensive blacklisting over a whole range of services and, especially with covert dataveillance, little or no chance to correct mistakes (and note that, in the UK legislation, there is a stated presumption that the information in the national ID register is correct). This procedure runs counter to the system of 'due process' long embodied in UK law and those systems of jurisprudence derived from it, for example those of the USA and Canada.

Very few people collecting data today are working towards nefarious ends; most are simply doing their job, often with the laudable intention of increasing efficiency within their business or government department. It is not data collection that is the primary concern, but the amount and extent of data now being collected and its *collation* within ever-more-massive databases. What safeguards should society demand in order to allay privacy concerns?

Codes and standards of behaviour have been suggested. These are well and good, but even when rigorously implemented they serve only to protect against individual 'rogue operators', those who would sell confidential information for gain, or attempt blackmail. The real cause for concern lies in institutional surveillance of individuals or groups.

Laws, regulations and privacy commissions are the normal route to counter government and corporate snooping. There is no doubt that such methods can prevent some of the worst excesses of a surveillance society – they can outlaw questionable practices; allow citizens the right to view (and correct) some of the files held on them; cause the formation of various oversight bodies to ensure regulations are adhered to, and to adjudicate on 'progress' in the field. But these solutions will work only if the political will to implement such legislation is present. And without detailed public knowledge of surveillance techniques, and of the extent to which they are being deployed, the groundswell of opinion necessary to drive a demand for such legislation will remain lacking.

The problem is that there will always be a perceived trade-off between security/efficiency and the privacy/autonomy of the individual. Powerful groups will advocate the former, while defenders of personal privacy must always remain at a financial and logistical disadvantage. There will be strong voices raised for increased surveillance to bolster tax revenue and discover tax cheats; to monitor illegal immigration; and most emotive of all, in these post 9/11 and 7/7 days, to counter terrorist aggression. There is no doubt that we face such internal and external threats, and that measures must be taken to neutralise them as far as is possible. But the opportunity this gives certain vested interests to use these legitimate concerns to advance an unacceptable level of surveillance across the whole of our society must also be recognised. There is an inverse relationship between this type of surveillance and personal privacy/freedom – as surveillance increases, freedom and privacy inevitably decline. For make no mistake, total security demands total surveillance.

An efficient means of curtailing domestic violence would undoubtedly be to have CCTV in every room of every house in the land, with each camera monitored 24/7. Or, better still, a government-authorised observer outside every window. Family violence would nose-dive, because any wrongdoing would be noted at its inception. But then again, so would every other move one made: eating, reading, staring at the ceiling, making love, nose-picking, taking a shower. All those private moments, sacrificed for the undoubtedly laudable end of fewer injured human beings. Who among us would agree to such a strategy?

The real question is: how much surveillance is too much? When is the cure worse than the disease? How much risk and inconvenience are we prepared to accept in order to preserve our liberties and our privacy? If this problem is not confronted openly by everyone in society, we face the likelihood of surveillance-creep, with the future a frightening mélange of Kafka-esque and Orwellian nightmares in which we have lost the freedoms we now so cherish. Ultimately we will get the surveillance, and the society, we deserve.

REFERENCES

Chapter 1

1 'United States Visitor and Immigrant Status Indicator Technology (US-VISIT)', Electronic Privacy Information Centre (EPIC), 2006; see http://www.epic.org/privacy/us-visit/

Chapter 2

1 'The Surveillance Society', *Wired* magazine, issue 9.12 (December 2001).
2 J. Bentham, *Proposal for a New and Less Expensive mode of Employing and Reforming Convicts* (London, 1798).
3 Ibid.

Chapter 3

1 Deuteronomy 1:22, *The Bible* (New International Version).
2 Letter 380, Kouyunjik Collection, rooms 2, 3. I.V. Harper, editor (1896), from L. Waterman, *The Royal Correspondence of the Assyrian Empire* (University of Michigan Press, 1930).
3 C. Dandeker, *Surveillance, Power and Modernity* (Polity Press, 1990).
4 M. Ignatieff, 'State, Civil Society and Total Institutions: a Critique of Recent Social Histories of Punishment', in S. Cohen and A. Scull, *Social Control and the State*, (Blackwell Publishing, 1985).

5 A.J.P. Taylor, *English History 1914-1945* (Oxford University Press, 1965), pp. 1-3.
6 T. Garton Ash, *The File: A Personal History* (Vintage Books, 1997).
7 D. Lyons (ed.), *Theorising Surveillance: the panopticon and beyond* (Uffculme: Willan Publishing, 2006).
8 BBC Radio 4, *Desert Island Discs*, 10 June 2007.

Chapter 4

1 Press release, 30 November 2004.
2 Meeting organised by Privacy International: see http://www.publictechnology.net
3 http://www.homeoffice.gov.uk/science-research/using-science/dna-database/
4 See for example http://www.ccc.de/biometrie/fingerabdruck_kopieren.xml?language=en
5 *House of Commons Official Report*, 25 January 2007, vol. 455, column 1567.
6 http://www.heise.de/ct/english/02/11/114/
7 http://www.leavethemkidsalone.com/facts-2.htm
8 http://www.leavethemkidsalone.com/docs/do_biometrics_have_a_place_in_school_3.pdf
9 'School fingerprints under the microscope' at http://www.leavethemkidsalone.com/security.htm, 2006.
10 R. Evison, 'School fingerprinting data security concerns', at http://www.leavethemkidsalone.com/docs/scenario.htm
11 www.timesonline.co.uk, 4 March 2007.
12 www.telegraph.co.uk, 9 April 2007.
13 http://www.lse.ac.uk/collections/pressAndInformationOffice/newsAndEvents/archives/2005/IDCard_FinalReport.htm
14 http://news.bbc.co.uk/1/hi/uk_politics/7084560.stm
15 http://www.no2id.net/IDSchemes/whyNot.php
16 http://www. epolitix.com/EN/MPWebsites/Lynne+Jones/bbd5635e-7073-4e26-bb7f-cd0252780200.htm
17 *Smartcard News*, vol. 16 (1), January 2007.
18 J. Fishenden, *The Scotsman*, 18 October 2005; also http://ntouk.com/archives/2005/Oct/18.10.2005.htm

19 *The Scotsman*, 18 October 2005; also
    http://ntouk.com/archives/2005/Oct/18.10.2005.htm
20 D.M. Wood (ed.), 'A Report on the Surveillance Society for the
    Information Commissioner by the Surveillance Studies Network',
    2006, paragraph 11.2.6.

Chapter 5

1   'Radio Frequency IDentification: applications and implications for
    consumers. A workshop report from the staff of the Federal Trade
    Commission', March 2005, p. 11.
2   'RFID Position Statement of Consumer Privacy and Civil Liberties
    Organizations' at http://www.privacyrights.org/ar/RFIDposition.htm,
    posted 20 November 2003.
3   Sun Microsystems, 'The Sun Global RFID Network Vision:
    Connecting Businesses at the Edge of the Network', a technical
    White Paper, July 2004.
4   http://www.ananova.com/news/story/
    sm_958267.html?menu=news.technology
5   T. Lewan at www.washingtonpost.com, 'Chip Implants Linked to
    Animal Tumors', 8 September 2007 (Associated Press).
6   J. Lettice at www.theregister.co.uk, '"RFID tag" the rude words ID
    Card ministers won't say', 30 January 2006.
7   B. Schneier, 'Fatal Flaw Weakens RFID Passport', *Wired*, November
    2005.
8   J. Lettice, op. cit.
9   *Guardian Unlimited* special report at www.guardian.co.uk,
    11 July 2006.
10 Statement of Barry Steinhardt, Director of the ACLU's Technology
    and Liberty Project on RFID tags before the Commerce, Trade and
    Consumer Protection Subcommittee of the House of Representatives
    Committee on Energy and Commerce, 14 July 2004.

Chapter 6

1 G. Armstrong and R. Giulianotti in C. Norris, J. Moran and G. Armstrong (eds.), *Surveillance, Closed Circuit Television and Social Control* (Brookfield: Ashgate Publishing, 1998).

2 A. Reeve in C. Norris, J. Moran and G. Armstrong (eds.), op. cit.

3 M. Clarke, 'Blind Eye on the Street' in *Police Review*, 5 August 1994.

4 C. Hale, 'Fear of Crime: A Review of the Literature', *International Review of Victimology*, vol. 4, 1996, pp. 79-150.

5 M. McCahill and C. Norris, 'Estimating the extent, sophistication and legality of CCTV in London', in M. Gill (ed.), *CCTV* (Leicester: Perpetuity Press, 2003).

6 C. Norris and G. Armstrong, *The Maximum Surveillance Society: The Rise of Closed Circuit Television* (Oxford: Oxford University Press, 1999).

7 N. Taylor, 'Closed Circuit Television: the British Experience', in *Stanford Technology Law Review*, vol. 11, 1999.

8 S. Davies, *Big Brother* (London: Pan Books, 1997), p. 182.

9 ACLU, 'What's Wrong With Public Video Surveillance?', at http://www.aclu.org/privacy/spying/14863res20020225.html

10 www.telegraph.co.uk/arts/main.jhtml?xml=/arts/2004/05/14/ftcctv14.xml

11 Quoted in S. Davies, op. cit.

12 'CCTV: a new battleground for privacy', in C. Norris, J. Moran and G. Armstrong (eds.), op. cit., p. 246.

13 Story from the *Daily Telegraph*, at http://www.theregister.co.uk/2004/06/18/blaggers_lift_cctv_cameras/

14 BioVision96, at http://www.dti-mi.org.uk/newweb/scid.htm. PNA report, *BioVision: Roadmap for Biometrics In Europe to 2010*, available at http://ftp.cwi.nl/CWIreports/PNA/PNA-E0303.pdf

15 See http://www.urban75.com/Action/cctv.html

16 See for example L. Wang, W.M. Hu, and T.N. Tan, 'Recent Developments in Human Motion Analysis', *Pattern Recognition*, vol. 36, no. 3, 2003, pp. 585-601.

17 *ANPR Strategy for the Police Service, 2005/2008*, 'Denying Criminals the Use of the Roads' section 4, March 2005.

18 D. Miles, American Forces Press Service, 3 January 2006:
    http://www.defenselink.mil/news/newsarticle.aspx?id=14711

Chapter 7

1 In J. Gleick, 'The End of Cash', at http://www.around.com/
   money.html (first published in the *New York Times Magazine*,
   16 June 1996).
2 http://news.digitaltrends.com/news/story/4484/phones_become_
   all-purpose_payment_devices
3 See http://www.spy.org.uk/cgi-bin/childlocate.pl
4 FollowUs website:
   http://www.followus.co.uk/how_accurate_is_it.html
5 http://jya.com/cell-track.htm
6 M. Smith, *The Killer Elite – The Inside Story of America's Most
   Secret Special Operations Team* (London: Cassell Guides, 2006).
7 *Observer*, 14 October 2002.
8 Defense Advanced Research Projects Agency (DARPA), 'Combat
   Zones That See' Broad Agency Announcement 03-15.

Chapter 8

1 L. Sherriff, 'Police slap cuffs on Punk SMSer', 3 June 2004, at
   http://www.theregister.co.uk/2004/06/03/text_punk/
2 D. Campbell, 'BT condemned for listing cables to US SIGINT
   station', *New Statesman*, 4 September 1997.
3 D. Ball and J. Richardson, *The Ties That Bind: intelligence
   cooperation between the UKUSA countries* (Boston: Allen &
   Unwin, 1985), pp. 223–4.
4 'Echelon, the NSA's global spying network', *Nexus Magazine*,
   August/September 1999, p. 21.
5 Quoted in J. Bamford, 'NSA, the Agency That Could Be Big
   Brother' in the *New York Times*, 25 December 2005.
6 'Echelon, the NSA's global spying network', *Nexus Magazine*,
   August/September 1999, p. 18.
7 See http://www.security.itworld.com/4361/040517euechelon/
   page_1.html

8 'Digital Security and Privacy for Human Rights Defenders', International Foundation for the Protection of Human Rights Defenders, at http://info.frontlinedefenders.org/manual/en/esecman/index.html?q=manual/en/esecman/

9 'The Threats to Privacy', Privacy International's Privacy and Human Rights Report 2004.

10 C. Williams, 'Chinese Reporter Targets Yahoo! From Prison Cell', 11 June 2007, at http://www.theregister.com/2007/06/11/yahoo_shi_tao_case/

11 'How Web Servers' Cookies Threaten Your Privacy' at http://www.junkbusters.com/cookies.html

Chapter 9

1 Beverly Dennis et al. v. Metromail et al., No. 96-04451, Travis County, Texas, USA.

2 'Privacy & Consumer Profiling', Electronic Privacy Information Centre (EPIC), 13 October 2004.

3 Quoted in CASPIAN: http://www.nocards.org/news/index.shtml#seg3

4 Ibid.

5 E. Schuman, 'A Smarter Smart Cart?' in eweek.com, 15 February 2005.

Chapter 10

1 R. Clarke, 'Dataveillance: delivering "1984"', in L. Green and R. Guinery (eds.), *Framing Technology: Society, Choice and Change* (Sydney: Allen & Unwin, 1994).

2 R. Clarke, 'Information Technology and Dataveillance', in C. Dunlop and R. Kling (eds.), *Controversies in Computing* (Academic Press, 1991).

3 R. Clarke, 'Dataveillance: delivering "1984"', in L. Green and R. Guinery (eds.), *Framing Technology: Society, Choice and Change* (Sydney: Allen & Unwin, 1994).

4 S. Davies, *Big Brother* (London: Pan Books, 1997), p. 87.

5 'The Identity Cards Bill – the Information Commissioner's Perspective', from the Information Commissioner's Office, at http://www.ico.gov.uk/upload/documents/library/corporate/ detailed_specialist_guides/id_cards_bill_ico_perspective_dec_2004.pdf

6 B. Hayes, 'SIS II: fait accompli? Construction of EU's Big Brother Database Underway', Statewatch analysis, May 2005.

7 '"Terrorism" Information Awareness (TIA)', at http://www.epic.org/privacy/profiling/tia/

8 American Civil Liberties Union, see http://www.aclu.org/privacy/spying/15324prs20050415.html

Chapter 11

1 M. Weiser, 'The computer for the 21st century', in *Scientific American*, 265 (September 1991), pp. 94–104.

2 S. Davies, *Big Brother* (London: Pan Books, 1997).

3 D. Lyon (ed.), 'Surveillance Studies: understanding visibility, mobility and the phenetic fix,' *Surveillance & Society* 1(1), pp. 1–7, available at www.surveillance-and-society.org

4 D. McKittrick, S. Kelters, B. Feeney, C. Thornton, D. McVea (eds.), *Lost Lives: the story of the men women and children who died as a result of the Northern Ireland Troubles* (Manchester: Trafalgar Press, 2001).

5 B. O'Brien, *The Long War – The IRA and Sinn Féin* (Dublin: O'Brien Press, 1999).

6 J. Toland, *Infamy: Pearl Harbor and its Aftermath* (New York: Berkley Books, 1983).

7 R. Stinnett, *Day of Deceit* (New York: Simon & Schuster, 2001).

8 'Pearl Harbor' at http://www.geocities.com/Pentagon/6315/ pearl.html

9 US Naval Institute Oral History Division, *The Reminiscences of Captain Joseph J. Rochefort*, 1970, p. 163.

10 *Rebuilding America's Defenses: Strategy, Forces and Resources for a New Century*. Report of The Project for the New American Century, September 2000.

11 *Justification for US Military Intervention in Cuba*, Annex to Appendix to enclosure A, 1962, suggestion nos. 8 and 4, pp. 10 and 8.

12 The Marriott Building also went down, but this was sited between

1 and 2 WTC, and was therefore subject to the worst effects of both collapses.

13 The interview can be heard on http://noonehastodie.blogspot.com/ 2007/06/jason-bermas-reveals-his-own-wtc-7.html

14 Note that the announcement was 26 minutes before the collapse 'on air', but we must allow time for the news to come in to the news team, and be fed from there to the newscasters.

15 http://www.bbc.co.uk/foi/docs/historical_information/ archive_policies/media_management_policy _overview.htm#top

16 http://www.whatreallyhappened.com/bbc_wtc7_videos.html

17 The National Security Strategy of the United States of America, Sept 2002. Available at http://www.whitehouse.gov/nsc/nss.html.

18 G. Elmer and A. Opel, *Theorising Surveillance: the pahopticon and beyond* (Willan Publishing, 2006).

Chapter 12

1 The Royal Academy of Engineering, London, *Dilemmas of Privacy and Surveillance, Challenges of Technological Change*, March 2007, section 5.1, p. 29.

2 The European Data Protection Directive 95/46/EC, no. 281, p. 12.

3 The Royal Academy of Engineering, op. cit., p. 30.

4 Ibid., p. 32.

5 D.M. Wood (ed.), *A Report on the Surveillance Society*, for the Information Commissioner by the Surveillance Studies Network, 2006, paragraph 44.7.

Chapter 13

1 H. Kennedy, *Just Law* (London: Vintage Books, 2004).

2 D.M. Wood (ed.), *A Report on the Surveillance Society*, for the Information Commissioner by the Surveillance Studies Network, 2006, paragraph 11.3.3.

3 M. Lianos, 'Social control after Foucault', in *Surveillance & Society* 1(3), 2003, pp. 412–30, available at http://www.surveillance-and-society.org/articles1(3)/AfterFoucault.pdf

4 R.V. Ericson and C.D. Shearing, 1986, in G. Marx, 'Technology

and Social Control: the Search for the Illusive Silver Bullet', in *The International Encyclopedia of the Social and Behavioural Sciences* (Pergamon, 2001).
5 D. Wood (ed.), op. cit., paragraph 11.4.3.
6 J. Lettice, 'DHS and UK ID Card Biometric Vendor in False ID Lawsuit', 11 May 2004, at http://www.theregister.co.uk/2004/05/11/identix_false_id_suit/
7 PRWeb press release newswire, 'Fingerprint Misidentification Victims File Class Action Lawsuit Against Identix, Oregon and Top State Law Enforcement Officials', 22 July 2004, at http://www.prweb.com/releases/2004/7/prweb143052.htm
8 H. Kennedy, op. cit.

Chapter 14

1 http://www.witness.org/index.php?Itemid=178&alert_id=20&option=com_rightsalert&task=view
2 'The price of freedom is eternal vigilance.' Thomas Jefferson, third president of the United States, 1801–09. Often used out of context, it was originally meant as a warning that the American people should closely watch their government to prevent excessive encroachment on personal liberty.
3 The Royal Academy of Engineering, London, *Dilemmas of Privacy and Surveillance, Challenges of Technological Change*, March 2007. See also www.ingeniatechnology.com
4 Ibid.
5 L. Lessig, *Code and Other Laws of Cyberspace* (New York, NY: Basic Books, 1999).
6 R. Clarke, 'Introducing PITs and PETs: Technologies Affecting Privacy', in *Privacy Law and Policy Reporter*, 7.9, 2001.
7 B. Stewart, 'Privacy impact assessments', in *Privacy Law and Policy Reporter*, 3 (4), 1996, pp. 61–4.
8 B. Stewart, 'PIAs – an early warning system', in *Privacy Law and Policy Reporter*, 3 (7), 1996, pp. 134–8.
9 P. Regan, *Legislating Privacy: Technology, Social Values, and Public Policy* (Chapel Hill: University of North Carolina Press, 1995).
10 D.M. Wood (ed.), *A Report on the Surveillance Society*, for the

Information Commissioner by the Surveillance Studies Network, 2006, paragraph 45.2.4.

11 'South Downs Earth First!', 1997. Cited in S. Davies, 'CCTV: a new battleground for privacy', in C. Norris, J. Moran and G. Armstrong (eds.), *Surveillance, Closed Circuit Television and Social Control* (Brookfield: Ashgate Publishing, 1998), p. 249.

12 SQUALL journal, 1997. Cited in S. Davies, 'CCTV: a new battleground for privacy', in C. Norris, J. Moran and G. Armstrong (eds.), op. cit., p. 250.

13 K.D. Haggerty and R. V. Ericson, 'The Surveillant Assemblage', in *British Journal of Sociology*, 51, 2000, pp. 605–22.

INDEX